JESUS: THE LAST DAY

A COLLECTION OF ESSAYS PUBLISHED BY
THE BIBLICAL ARCHAEOLOGY SOCIETY

— Contributors —
Dan Bahat
Bruce Chilton
Jerome Murphy-O'Connor
Thomas Schmidt
Hershel Shanks
Joan Taylor
Vassilios Tzaferis

— Editor —
Molly Dewsnap Meinhardt

On the Cover: Christ Carrying the Cross,
by Gian Francesco de' Maineri (fl. 1489-1506).
Collection: Galleria e Museo Estense, Modena, Italy;
Photo by Bridgeman Art Library.

Library of Congress Cataloging-in-Publication Data

Jesus : the last day / editor, Molly Dewsnap Meinhardt;
contributors, Dan Bahat ... [et al.].
p. cm.
Includes bibliographical references.
1. Jesus Christ--Biography--Passion Week. 2. Bible. N.T. Gospels--Antiquities.
I. Meinhardt, Molly Dewsnap. II. Bahat, Dan.
BT414.J47 2003
232.96--dc21
2003011780

© 2003 Biblical Archaeology Society
4710 41st St., NW
Washington, DC 20016

All essays previously appeared in *Biblical Archaeology Review* or *Bible Review*

Design by Francis Sheehan
ISBN 1-880317-63-X

TABLE OF CONTENTS

INTRODUCTION

The Gospels focus intensely on Jesus' last days. Almost a third of the Gospel of Mark is devoted to the final week of Jesus' life. A third of the Gospel of John covers just one day, the day of his death.

According to Matthew, Mark and Luke, this final day begins when Jesus sends his disciples into Jerusalem to prepare a Passover meal before the sun sets. It will be Jesus' last meal with his followers. Twenty-four hours later, Jesus is crucified. Before the sun sets again, Joseph of Arimathea wraps the corpse in a linen shroud and lays it in a rock-cut tomb.

In the Jewish tradition into which Jesus was born, raised and died, the new day begins at sundown. Thus these last 24 hours are truly one day in the life of Jesus. In a sense, however, this is not his *last* day; Jesus' story continues beyond the tomb, which is precisely why this day was selected as the focal point of both the Gospels and this slim book.

Each of the following essays is devoted to one event in this pivotal day. Each approaches the text from a different angle. A deeper knowledge of first-century Jewish ritual practice allows for a more accurate reading of Jesus' famous words—"This is my body, this is my flesh"—at the Last Supper. Archaeology helps pinpoint the location of Gethsemane, where Jesus prayed to his Father the night before he died, and of Golgotha, where he was crucified. A literary portrait of Mark as a skilled writer addressing a very specific audience helps us understand why he told the story as he did. The agony Jesus suffered on the cross is made palpable through recent medical research into the physiological effects of crucifixion.

The essay on Mark (Chapter 4) offers an important message to modern Bible readers: The gospel writers did not have us in mind when they wrote their books. They were writing for specific historical audiences. To understand what they were trying to say, we must learn what their message meant in Jerusalem or Rome or Antioch in the first century. We hope each of these essays will bring you closer to that first-century world, and thus closer to what the gospel writers were really saying about Jesus' last day.

Molly Dewsnap Meinhardt
Washington, D.C.

Acknowledgments

Many thanks are due to Kenneth M. Kerr for thinking of a book like this, Francis Sheehan for designing it, Julia Bozzolo for creating the maps, and Hilary Metternich, Bonnie Mullin and Sara Murphy for carefully proofreading the text.

About the Authors

DAN BAHAT served as Jerusalem district archaeologist for the government of Israel from 1978 to 1990; before that he was the district archaeologist for the Galilee. Bahat has directed digs at Tel Dan, the Beth-Shean synagogue and Herod's Palace in Jerusalem. In 1989 he became the third person ever to receive the prestigious Jerusalem Award for Archaeology.

BRUCE CHILTON is the Bernard Iddings Bell Professor of Religion at Bard College, director of the college's Institute of Advanced Theology and rector of the Church of St. John the Evangelist, in Barrytown, New York. He is the author of several books, including *The Isaiah Targum* (1987), the first critical translation of the Aramaic version of Isaiah, *Rabbi Jesus: An Intimate Biography* (2000) and, most recently, *Redeeming Time* (2002).

JEROME MURPHY-O'CONNOR, O.P., a professor of New Testament and intertestamental literature, has taught at the École Biblique et Archéologique in Jerusalem for more than 30 years. He is the author of the popular little blue guidebook *The Holy Land: An Archaeological Guide*, now in its fourth edition from Oxford University Press, and of *Paul: A Critical Life* (1996).

THOMAS SCHMIDT, a specialist in New Testament ethics, formerly taught at Westmont College and now teaches at the Laguna Blanca School. He is author of *A Scandalous Beauty: The Artistry of God and the Way of the Cross* (2002) and *Straight & Narrow?: Compassion & Clarity in the Homosexuality Debate* (1995).

HERSHEL SHANKS is editor of *Bible Review, Biblical Archaeology Review, Archaeology Odyssey* and *Moment* magazines. He is the author of *The Brother of Jesus* (with Ben Witherington III, 2003), *The Mystery and Meaning of the Dead Sea Scrolls* (1998) and *Jerusalem: An Archaeological Biography* (1995).

JOAN E. TAYLOR is author of *Beneath the Church of the Holy Sepulchre* (with Shimon Gibson, 1994), *Jerusalem: The Archaeology and Early History of Traditional Golgotha* (1994) and *The Immerser: John the Baptist Within Second Temple Judaism* (1997).

VASSILIOS TZAFERIS recently retired as director of excavations and surveys at the Israel Antiquities Authority. Tzaferis directed digs at Kursi, Shepherd's Field (Bethlehem), Tiberias, Ashkelon, Beth-Shean and Capernaum.

CHAPTER ONE

WHAT JESUS DID AT
THE LAST SUPPER

Bruce Chilton

What Jesus was doing at the Last Supper has not been understood for the better part of 2,000 years. The reason for the misunderstanding is that Jesus, a Jewish teacher who was concerned with the sacrificial worship of Israel, has been treated as if he were instead the deity in a Hellenistic cult.

Within a generation after Jesus' death, when the Gospels were written, non-Jews had come to predominate in the Church. The Romans had destroyed the Jerusalem Temple (in 70 C.E.);* the most influential centers of Christianity were cities of the Mediterranean world such as Alexandria, Antioch, Corinth, Damascus, Ephesus and Rome. Although large numbers of Jews were also followers of Jesus, non-Jews controlled how the Gospels were written after 70 C.E. and how the texts were interpreted.

Within the Greco-Roman world, Jesus was readily appreciated as a divine figure, after the manner of one of the gods come to visit earth.

*B.C.E. (Before the Common Era) and C.E. (Common Era) are alternative designations for B.C. and A.D. often used in scholarly literature.

Hellenistic religion of the first and second centuries was deeply influenced by cults called *Mysteries*, in which a worshiper would be joined to the death and restoration of a god by means of ritual. Jesus' Last Supper was naturally compared to initiation into such a Mystery. He was a new kind of Dionysus, historical rather than mythical, who gave himself, flesh and blood, in the meals held in his name. After all, he had said, "This is my body" and "This is my blood" (Matthew 26:26-28//Mark 14:22-24//Luke 22:19-20). For many Hellenistic Christians, this could only mean that Jesus was referring to himself: Bread and wine were tokens of Jesus that became his body and blood when believers consumed them!

The only serious question for Christian orthodoxy was how the transformation took place. Churches have gone to war (literally and figuratively) over that issue, but they have agreed that the meaning of body and blood is self-referential, or autobiographical; that is, Jesus was talking about himself, about his own flesh and his own blood.

This traditional understanding has gone virtually unchallenged, both in theological and in historical discussion. Churches have accepted the idea that the Last Supper initiated a Mystery religion in which God gave himself to be eaten. Historians have told us that Jesus started a new sect of Judaism by telling his followers to eat bread and drink wine as if they were his own flesh and blood.

But is that plausible as history? What Jew would tell another to drink blood, even symbolic blood? When the Mishnah* presents an example of heinous *defect* on the part of a priest involved in the slaughtering of the red heifer, it describes the priest as intending to eat the flesh or drink the blood (*Parah* 4:3). In fact, in Jewish tradition, people had no share of blood; that belonged only to God. The thought of drinking blood, even animal blood, was blasphemous. To imagine drinking human blood and consuming it with human flesh could only make the blasphemy worse.

---

*The Mishnah is an early compilation of Jewish oral law dating from about 200 C.E.

So if Jesus' words are taken with their traditional, autobiographical meaning, his Last Supper can only be understood as a deliberate break from Judaism. Either Jesus himself declared a new religion or his followers did so in his name and invented the Last Supper themselves. Both those alternatives find scholarly adherents, and the debate between those who see the Gospels as true, literal reports and those who see them as literary fictions shows little sign of abating.

There is, however, a more historical way of understanding how the Eucharist emerged in early Christianity, an approach that takes account of cultural changes in the development of the movement.

Research in the social world of early Judaism indicates how Christianity emerged as a social movement within Judaism and then became distinct from it. We are no longer faced with the old alternatives—either the conservative position that the Gospels are literal reports or the liberal position that they are literary fictions. Critical study has suggested a new possibility: that the Gospels are composite products of various social groups that belonged to the Jesus movement from its days within Judaism until its emergence as a distinct religion known as Christianity. By understanding Eucharistic practice within the social groups that made the Gospels into the texts we read today, we can begin to appreciate the meaning Jesus gave to the Last Supper and then trace how his original meaning was later transformed.

The Synoptic Gospels (Mark, Matthew and Luke) were composed by successive groups of teachers after Jesus' death in about 30 C.E.* The Gospel of Mark was the first, written around 71 C.E. in the environs of Rome, according to most scholars. Matthew was next in about 80 C.E., perhaps in Damascus (or elsewhere in Syria). Luke came later, say in 90 C.E., perhaps in Antioch.

*The first three Gospels are called "Synoptic," from the Greek for "seeing together," because they can be viewed together when they are printed in columns. Judaic documents also present synoptic relationships, but the similar *order* of passages in the Synoptic Gospels is especially striking. In my judgment, that common order reflects a widely used model of baptismal instruction within the early Church.

Some of the teachers who shaped the Gospels shared Jesus' cultural milieu, but others never set eyes on him; they lived far from Judea at a later period and were not practicing Jews. The growth of Christianity involved a rapid transition from culture to culture and, within each culture, from subculture to subculture. A basic prerequisite for understanding any text of the Gospels, therefore, is to define the cultural context of a given statement. That is just what the usual reading of the Last Supper fails to do.

The Last Supper was not the *only* supper Jesus shared with his disciples—just the last one. Indeed, Jesus had a well-established custom of eating with people socially. There was nothing unusual about a rabbi making social eating an instrument of his instruction, and so it was part of Jesus' method from the first days of his movement in Galilee.

Meals within Judaism were regular expressions of social solidarity and of common identity as the people of God. Many sorts of meals are mentioned in the literature of early Judaism. From the Dead Sea Scrolls, we learn of banquets at which the community convened in order of hierarchy. Among the Pharisees, collegial meals were shared within fellowships (*havuroth*) at which like-minded fellows (*haverim*) shared food and company they considered pure. Ordinary households might welcome the coming of the Sabbath with a prayer of sanctification (*kiddush*) over a cup of wine. Families also might begin celebrations with blessings (*berakhot*) over the bread and wine.

Jesus' meals were in some ways similar but in other ways distinctive. He had a special understanding of what the meal meant and of who should participate. For him, eating socially with others in Israel was a parable of the feast in the kingdom that was to come. A key feature of the fervent expectations of Judaism during the first century was that in the kingdom to come God would offer festivity for all peoples on his holy mountain (see, for example, Isaiah 25:6-8). Jesus shared that hope, as we see in the following passage.

> Many shall come from east and west,
> and feast with Abraham, Isaac, and Jacob
> in the kingdom of God.
> > (Matthew 8:11//Luke 13:28-29)*

Eating was a way of enacting the kingdom of God, of practicing the generous rule of the divine king.

Jesus' meals were also distinctive in that they were inclusive; he avoided any exclusive practices that would divide the people of God from one another. He accepted all the people of God as meal companions—including tax agents and other suspicious characters—and even received notorious sinners at his table. The meal for him was a sign of the kingdom of God, and all Israelites, assuming they sought forgiveness, were to have access to it.

Jesus' practice of fellowship at meals caused opposition from those whose understanding of Israel was exclusive. To them, he seemed profligate, willing to eat and drink with anyone, as Jesus observed in another passage:

> A man came eating and drinking,
> and they complain:
> Look, a glutton and drunkard,
> a fellow of tax agents and sinners.
> > (Matthew 11:19//Luke 7:34)

Jesus' opponents saw the purity of Israel as something that could be guarded only by separating from others, as at meals. Jesus' view of

---

*In this essay, I cite Jesus' sayings according to my reconstruction of the Aramaic behind the Gospels. In each case, I provide reference to the passages on which my reconstruction is based. This saying is from the source scholars call Q (short for German *Quelle*, or "source"), which is an early collection of Jesus' sayings that were incorporated into the Gospels of Matthew and Luke, often in nearly identical language. But the variations between Matthew and Luke show that Q was not a fixed written source.

purity was different. He held that a son or daughter of Israel, by virtue of being Israel, could approach his table and also worship in God's Temple. (Consider the story of Jesus declaring a "leper" clean [Matthew 8:14//Mark 1:40-45] and the story of the woman with the ointment [Luke 7:36-50].) Repentance could be required—Jesus taught his followers to pray for forgiveness daily—but in his understanding all Israelites were pure and fit to offer purely of their own within the sacrificial worship of Israel.

Jesus' views led to disputes in Galilee, but these were only of local interest. (Slightly deviant rabbis were far from uncommon there, which is why the region is referred to as "Galilee of the nations" in Isaiah 9:1.) But when Jesus brought his teaching to the Jerusalem Temple, where he insisted on his own teaching (or *halakhah*) of purity, matters were different. The resulting dispute is reflected in an incident often called the cleansing of the Temple (Matthew 21:12-13//Mark 11:15-17//Luke 19:45-46//John 2:13-17). From the viewpoint of the authorities, what Jesus was after was the opposite of cleansing. He objected to the merchants who had permission to sell sacrificial animals in the vast outer court of the Temple. In Jesus' "peasant's" view of purity, Israel should not offer priests produce for which they paid money, but their own sacrifices that they themselves brought to the Temple. He believed this so vehemently that he and his followers drove the animals and the sellers out of the great court, apparently with the use of force (Matthew 21:12//Mark 11:15-16//Luke 19:45//John 2:15-16).

Jesus' interference in the ordinary worship of the Temple might have been sufficient in itself to bring about his execution. After all, for as long as it stood, the Temple was the center of Judaism. Roman officials were so interested in its smooth functioning at the hands of the priests they appointed that they were known to sanction the death penalty for gross sacrilege.[1] Yet there is no indication that Jesus was arrested immediately. Instead, he remained at liberty for some time and was finally taken into custody just after one of his meals, the Last Supper (Matthew 26:47-56//Mark 14:43-52//Luke 22:47-53; John 18:3-11).

The decision of the Temple authorities to move against Jesus when they did is what made it the final supper.

Why did the authorities wait? And why did they act when they did?

The Gospels portray the authorities as fearful of the popular backing Jesus enjoyed (Matthew 26:5//Mark 14:2//Luke 22:2; John 11:47-48), and his inclusive teaching of purity probably did bring enthusiastic followers into the Temple with him.

But there was another factor: Jesus could not simply be dispatched as a cultic criminal. He was not attempting an onslaught upon the Temple as such; his dispute with the authorities concerned purity within the Temple. Other rabbis of his period also engaged in physical demonstrations regarding purity in the conduct of worship. One of them, for example, is said once to have driven thousands of sheep *into* the Temple, so that people could offer sacrifice in the manner he approved (Babylonian Talmud, *Beza* 20a-b). Jesus' action was extreme but not totally without precedent, even in the use of force.

The authorities' delay, then, was understandable. We might even say it was commendable, reflecting continued controversy over the merits of Jesus' teaching and whether his occupation of the Temple's Great Court should be condemned.

Why then did they finally arrest Jesus?

The Last Supper provides the key. Something about Jesus' meals after his occupation of the Temple caused Judas to inform on Jesus. ("Judas" is the only name New Testament traditions have left us. Exactly which or how many of Jesus' disciples became disaffected after his occupation of the Temple cannot be known with any certainty.) Jesus' meals had never been private, and any new meaning he gave them would quickly have become known in the tense period after his occupation of the Temple.

However they learned of Jesus' new interpretation of his meals of fellowship, the authorities arrested him just after the supper we call last. After his "cleansing" of the Temple, Jesus continued to celebrate fellowship at table as a foretaste of the kingdom, just as he had before.

But he added a new and scandalous dimension of meaning. His occupation of the Temple having failed, Jesus said over the wine, "This is
my blood," and over the bread, "This is my flesh" (Matthew
26:26,28//Mark 14:22,24//Luke 22:19-20; 1 Corinthians 11:24-25;
Justin, *Apology* 1.66.3).

In the context of his confrontation with the Temple authorities,
Jesus' words can have had only one meaning. He cannot have meant,
"Here are my personal body and blood"; that interpretation makes
sense only at a later stage in the development of Christianity. Jesus'
point rather was that, in the absence of a Temple permitting his view
of purity to be practiced, wine would be his blood of sacrifice, and
bread would be his flesh of sacrifice! When he said, "This is my blood,
this is my flesh," he meant that these—the wine and bread—were his
substitute sacrifices, replacing the blood and flesh of animals being
sacrificed at the Temple.

In Aramaic, "blood" (*dema*) and "flesh" (*bisra*, which may also
be rendered as "body") are words that can have a sacrificial meaning; in the context of Jesus' speech at the Last Supper, that is their
most natural meaning.

Jesus claimed that by sharing meals in anticipation of the kingdom, he and his followers offered more acceptable worship than
what was offered in the Temple. The wine was better blood, the
bread better flesh, than Temple sacrifices that were little more than
commercial devices.

The meaning of the Last Supper actually evolved over a series of
meals following Jesus' occupation of the Temple. During that period,
Jesus claimed that wine and bread were a better sacrifice than what
was offered in the Temple, a foretaste of new wine in the kingdom of
God (see Matthew 26:29//Mark 14:25). At least wine and bread were
Israel's own, not tokens of priestly dominance.

No wonder the opposition to him became deadly—even among
the twelve (in the shape of Judas, according to the Gospels): In essence,
Jesus made his meals into a rival altar.

This interpretation has two advantages over the traditional understanding of the words "This is my body, this is my blood." The first advantage is contextual: This interpretation places Jesus firmly within the Judaism of his period, and at the same time accounts for the opposition of the authorities to him. The second advantage is its explanatory power: It enables us to explain subsequent developments in the understanding of the Eucharist within early Christianity.

After Jesus' crucifixion, his followers were convinced that God had raised him from the dead. They were thus encouraged to continue the pattern of social eating Jesus had established. They even claimed that the risen Jesus was present during such meals (Luke 24:13-35,36-43; John 21:1-14).

Two groups especially influenced the way in which the Eucharist was understood within the early Church, prior to the time the Gospels were written. The first (chronologically) was the group around Peter; the second was the group around James, the brother of Jesus.

The Petrine group drew its support from members who were active in Jerusalem, Galilee and Syria; they conceived of Jesus as offering a fresh understanding of the covenant God had made with Israel. In stories like the Transfiguration (Matthew 17:1-9//Mark 9:2-10//Luke 9:28-36), Jesus is, in effect, portrayed as a new Moses. For the Petrine group this new Moses used wine to seal the covenant that his teaching conveyed. This is made explicit when Jesus is made to say, not simply "This is my blood," but "This is my blood *of the covenant.*" (See Matthew 26:28//Mark 14:24; compare Luke 22:20 and 1 Corinthians 11:25, which develop the thought still further: Jesus' blood becomes the seal of the "*new* covenant.")

In this interpretation, the blood and flesh are still not Jesus' own. They remain the equivalent of the Temple offering of animal sacrifices. They are an appropriate offering within Jesus' understanding of the covenant between God and his people. Remember that Moses had offered and sprinkled blood prior to giving the original covenant and even called it "the blood of the covenant" (Exodus 24:6-8). The Petrine group was simply following this tradition. But Moses did not use his own blood to seal the covenant: The very thought would have been repulsive. It is clear that the Petrine understanding of the Eucharist as covenantal is inconsistent with the notion that Jesus is referring to his own blood when he says, "This is my blood." For the Petrine group, the wine, representing blood, was the means of sacrificial confirmation, as in the case of Moses. The identification with Jesus' own blood was not yet made.

The circle of James, Jesus' brother, appears in almost every way to have been more conservative than the circle of Peter. Jesus' brother was not a prominent figure in the movement until after the crucifixion, but he quickly took over leadership of the Church in Jerusalem from Peter and insisted upon the central importance of worship in the Temple. James also insisted that the direction of the Church should be in the hands of practicing Jews, not under the control of teachers such as Paul who were willing to depart from Judaism (see Galatians 2 and Acts 21:17-36).

The circle of James, in keeping with its conservatism, contributed no language of its own to the words attributed to Jesus at the Last Supper, as the Petrine group did by referring to the "blood of the covenant," instead of simply retaining "This is my blood." But by other means the Jamesian group effected a tight restriction on who could rightly take part in the meal. They identified Jesus' Last Supper in precise terms with Passover; his final meal was a Seder, with all its attendant preparations (Matthew 26:17-20//Mark 14:12-17//Luke 22:7-14).

Recent scholarship has rightly seen that the identification of the Last Supper with Passover is theologically motivated. After all, the Gospels themselves have the authorities resolve to deal with Jesus *before* the crowds of Passover arrive (Matthew 26:1-5//Mark 14:1-2//Luke 22:1-2). The basic elements of the Seder—lamb, unleavened bread, bitter herbs (see Exodus 12:8)—are notably absent at the Last Supper. By identifying Jesus' Last Supper with the Passover meal, the Jamesian group managed to limit participation in the Eucharist to Jews, since circumcision was a strict requirement for males who took part in a Seder (Exodus 12:48-49).

Paul never accepted the limitation of the Jamesian group. He placed the Last Supper on the night Jesus was handed over, not on Passover (1 Corinthians 11:23). In that way, non-Jewish Christians—who were Paul's particular concern—could take part fully in the Lord's supper. Paul also adopted the Petrine group's understanding of the blood Jesus referred to at the Last Supper as the blood of the covenant. Quoting Jesus, Paul writes, "This cup is the new covenant in my blood" (1 Corinthians 11:25). Paul wrote 1 Corinthians around 56 C.E., so it is plain that by that time there were rich and varying understandings of the Eucharist. Like Luke (22:20), Paul believes the covenant mediated by Jesus is "new," a departure from old ways.

The Synoptic Gospels were written later than 70 C.E., but on the basis of earlier traditions. They reflect previous understandings of the Eucharist, but they also develop the personal interpretation, which then becomes normative. They do so in the Passion Narrative, the story of Jesus' last days.

The Passion Narrative (Matthew 26:1-27:61; Mark 14:1-15:47; Luke 22:1-23:55) is a source of early Christian teaching devised around 50 C.E. to educate converts in the Hellenistic world for baptism. The fact that the Passion Narrative focuses on Jesus' death is significant. Unlike the early source of Jesus' teaching, a collection of sayings known as Q, the Passion Narrative focuses on Jesus' biography at the point of his death. His death, rather than his words, best conveys his meaning for converts.

The close link between the Last Supper and Jesus' death assured that, in the Greco-Roman environment in which the Passion Narrative grew, the wine of the Eucharist that represented the blood of sacrifice was understood to be Jesus' own blood. In the Passion Narrative, written for non-Jews in the Hellenistic world, Jesus' blood was shed not only for Israel, but for "many," as Matthew 26:28 and Mark 14:24 have it, or for "you," as Luke 22:20 has Jesus express it. In either wording, an extension to include the non-Jewish audience of the Gospels is apparent.

The Passion Narrative was originally composed in Greek. The Greek term for "body" (*soma*), unlike its Aramaic antecedent, unequivocally meant "body," and not "flesh." By the time the Gospel tradition took form in Greek and in the Greek world—during the period when Paul was active—Jesus was understood in the Eucharist to be giving himself for the world, as was the case in the Passion Narrative. The wine as blood and the bread as flesh (now body) became Jesus' own blood and body.

It was but a short step to the theology of John's gospel (written around 100 C.E.), where eating Jesus' flesh and drinking his blood becomes a condition of eternal life:

> So Jesus said to him "Very truly, I tell you, unless you eat the flesh of the Son of Man and drink his blood, you have no life in yourselves. The one who consumes my flesh and drinks my blood has eternal life, and I will raise that one on the last day; for my flesh is true food and my blood is true drink. The one who consumes my flesh and drinks my blood abides in me, and I in that one. Just as the living Father sent me, and I live because of the Father, so whoever consumes me will live because of me."
>
> (John 6:53-57)

The Johannine Jesus makes the Eucharist into a Mystery: Each individual who takes bread and wine is joined to the divine flesh and blood that was offered in death and raised in triumph. The link between Jesus and the believer on a personal level is emphatic. "The one who consumes" his flesh (*ho trogon*, literally, "the one who chews and eats") is promised personal and permanent transformation by ingesting divine food.

The Eucharist developed within the Jesus movement from its earliest days until Christianity emerged as a religion distinct from Judaism. In order to understand Eucharistic texts, we need to be sensitive to the meanings associated with the various cultures and subcultures of early

Christianity. Those cultures and subcultures—each with its own meaning—generated the texts we read today. I call the analysis of the meanings that went into those texts the generative reading of the New Testament.[2]

The stages we have been able to trace, within Jesus' activity, within the circles of Peter and James, within the teaching of the Synoptic Gospels and finally within the Gospel of John, reflect practices and meanings of the Eucharist at distinct moments in the development of early Christianity. They are what generated the texts. At no stage, however, is there a desire simply to record what once happened in the fellowship of Jesus. The texts were not composed to satisfy historical curiosity.

One of the tests of a generative reading is whether the movement from one meaning to another during the development of a text can be explained. That test is met in the present case regarding Eucharistic practice. There is no need to suppose that a named or anonymous author simply concocted Eucharistic practice and convinced the Church to accept it. Rather, each successive community imputed to the Eucharist the form that corresponded to its own understanding of the meaning of that meal.

Sharing a festal meal was basic to Jesus' program. He invited all Israel to anticipate the kingdom with an assurance of their fitness to do so, and later claimed his meals were preferable to sacrifices at the Temple. The circle of Peter saw in Jesus' practice a confirmation of the covenant that was of Mosaic proportions. The circle of James believed that Passover among circumcised Jews was the ideal of Jesus' fellowship. By the time the Synoptic tradition was framed, teachers such as Paul had done their work, and the Eucharist was viewed as open to all who would follow in the footsteps of the self-giving martyred hero who made his body and blood available to his followers, just as in Hellenistic Mystery religions. In John the language of Mystery becomes emphatic and unmistakable.

The movement from one meaning to another was not a matter of invention. Each meaning reflects what the Eucharist represented for the community concerned, and each community formalized its understanding in its portrait of what Jesus did and said. That process is as natural as the development of liturgies throughout the history of the Church.

Only the persistent tendency to abstract the Gospels from history and practice can explain why modern discussion has split into a fruitless opposition between those who insist the Gospels simply relate what really happened and those who postulate literary innovators bent on fiction. Neither alternative is appealing. But we need not limit ourselves to them. Examining the generative meanings within texts can help us see how the practices of early Christianity produced distinctive understandings, in this case of Jesus' words at the Last Supper.

1. See Josephus, *The Antiquities* 15.417.

2. For a more extended analysis of the Eucharistic texts, see Bruce Chilton, *A Feast of Meanings: Eucharistic Theologies from Jesus Through Johannine Circles*, Supplements to *Novum Testamentum* (Leiden: Brill, 1994). In regard to Jesus' view of sacrifice, see Chilton, *The Temple of Jesus: His Sacrificial Program Within a Cultural History of Sacrifice* (University Park: Penn State Press, 1992).

CHAPTER TWO

WHERE WAS GETHSEMANE?

Joan E. Taylor

When visitors to Jerusalem are shown a large cave called Gethsemane on the lower slopes of the Mount of Olives, they usually give a perfunctory look and hurry on to the famous Garden of Gethsemane, the small garden of olive trees adjacent to the Church of All Nations. Here pilgrims can sit and reflect on the momentous events of Jesus' arrest in what seems a more appropriate, if less authentic, environment.

Most of these pilgrims are never told that the New Testament does not mention a *Garden* of Gethsemane. The Cave of Gethsemane, on the other hand, is very probably the location of Jesus' arrest and thus is a genuine Biblical site unlike so many of the "traditional" holy sites of Christianity that have little or no claim to authenticity.

The cave, within a property now owned by the Franciscan Custody for the Holy Land, certainly looks unimpressive. Enclosed in a flat-roofed, semicircular building, the cave is reached by a long corridor to the right of the courtyard leading to the traditional Tomb of the Virgin Mary. The entrance makes it seem an afterthought, though in fact the cave was a Christian holy site long before anyone thought

GARO NALBANDIAN

A grove of gnarled olive trees, reputedly more than 1,000 years old, thrives in what is today called the Garden of Gethsemane, located just outside the Church of All Nations, on the Mount of Olives. But although tradition locates Jesus' last night of anguished prayer in a garden, the Bible doesn't. It just mentions "a place called Gethsemane." The Hebrew name means "press of oils," leading author Taylor to suggest that Gethsemane was not a garden at all, but a nearby cave that housed an olive-oil press in Jesus' time.

to place the Tomb of the Virgin Mary beside it. The interior of the rather spartan cave has traces of two levels of Byzantine (fourth-sixth century) mosaics, intriguing medieval ceiling and wall decorations and modern altars on a modern stone floor. These features, however, do not seem too inspiring to most visitors and testify only to the fact that the cave has been modified many times over the course of its long history.

In the first century, the cave wasn't tucked behind a large building, as it is today. Excavations conducted by the Franciscans in 1956 and 1957 revealed that the natural mouth of the cave, lying to the north, was over 16 feet wide. The cave itself was much extended long before the Byzantine period and was used for agricultural purposes.

The earliest gospel, Mark, describes Jesus and his disciples going out to the Mount of Olives after the Last Supper (Mark 14:26) and specifically identifies their stopping place: "They went to a place called

Gethsemane" (Mark 14:32). Mark does not call it a garden but simply a "place" or "property," in Greek *chōrion*. Jesus asks his disciples to
sit down "here" (*hōde*) while he prays. He then "takes to himself"
(*paralambanei*) Peter, James and John. The Greek word implies that he
invites them to one side with him, not that he goes away with them
anywhere. Distressed, he asks the three to remain "here" (*hōde*) and
keep awake. The other disciples are presumably permitted to slumber,
but not the special three. Jesus goes "forward a little" (*proelthōn
mikron*), where he throws himself on the ground and asks that he
might avoid his fate. To "go forward" is perhaps a rather curious way
of referring to Jesus' departure. A little later, Mark makes it clear that
Jesus actually went away: "And again he went away (*apelthōn*) and
prayed, saying the same thing" (Mark 14:39). Jesus does this three
times and on returning always finds Peter, James and John asleep, and
asks them again to keep awake and pray. The last time he announces
that the hour of his betrayal has come. Then Judas arrives with an
armed crowd sent by the chief priests, scribes and elders of Jerusalem
and identifies his master by greeting him with the customary kiss.

Mark implies that, at the moment of betrayal, Jesus is not simply
with Peter, James and John but with all the disciples who came with
him across the Kidron Valley to Gethsemane. The armed crowd, carrying swords and clubs, seizes Jesus. One of the disciples standing
near Jesus draws his sword and cuts off the ear of a servant of the high
priest. A young man in the gathering, who seems to have been asleep
in nothing more than a linen cloth or undergarment, a *sindōn*,
attempts to follow Jesus as they take him away. The group sent by the
chief priests and scribes grabs hold of the young man who manages
to tear away, but unfortunately without his clothing (Mark 14:51); he
flees nude. Mark specifically notes that "everyone deserted him [Jesus]
and fled" (Mark 14:50). Jesus was therefore not simply with Peter,
James and John, but with the whole group of disciples.

Luke and Matthew, basing their accounts of the arrest on Mark,
have similar stories. Luke mentions that Jesus spent his nights "on the

Mount of Olives" (Luke 21:37) during the time he was in Jerusalem, but at first does not say exactly where. Matthew also refers to him sitting and teaching his disciples somewhere at a place on the Mount of Olives (Matthew 24:3). As in Mark, both Luke and Matthew refer to Jesus and his disciples going to the Mount of Olives after the Last Supper (Matthew 26:30; Luke 22:39). According to Matthew, Jesus goes with them to "a place named Gethsemane" (Matthew 26:36), but there is no mention of a garden. Luke never bothers to record the name of the place, but simply indicates it was where Jesus regularly slept: "He came out and went, as was his custom, to the Mount of Olives; and the disciples followed him. When he reached the place, he said to them, 'Pray that you may not come into the time of trial'" (Luke 22:39-40). Luke's account does not single out Peter, James and John. Jesus goes away from all his disciples about a "stone's throw" and prays. He returns only once, to find them all fast asleep, and asks them to get up and pray. Judas arrives, and the scene is the same as in Mark, apart from a few details: For example, Jesus heals the ear of the high priest's servant, the poor young man who lost his clothes is not mentioned and there is no direct reference to Jesus' disciples all running away. Matthew's story (Matthew 26:36-56) is very close to that of Mark, almost word for word, apart from a few minor changes and the subtraction of the tale of the naked man. Clearly both Luke and Matthew thought this detail anecdotal and irrelevant.[1]

Neither Mark, Matthew nor Luke speak of a garden. Gethsemane is simply a "place" or "property" on the Mount of Olives.

The Gospel of John, however, mentions something called a *kēpos*. *Kēpos* can be translated as "garden," but it is really a general term, more accurately translated as "a cultivated tract of land." It can refer to anything from a large orchard or plantation to a small plot. More importantly, John never calls this cultivated area (*kēpos*) Gethsemane. Only by conflating this account with the stories in Mark, Matthew and Luke did later Christians formulate such an idea. John's account goes like this: "After Jesus had spoken these words, he went out [from Jerusalem] with his disciples across the Kidron Valley to where there was a garden/cultivated area (*kēpos*), into which he and his disciples entered. Now Judas, who betrayed him, also knew the place, because Jesus met there often with his disciples" (John 18:1-2). John, like Luke, describes a place that Jesus frequented. Since it is nighttime, the implication is that he intended, as usual, to sleep there. John's gospel contains no story of Jesus' prayer. Judas simply arrives all of a sudden with soldiers and Temple police. In John, Judas does not kiss Jesus. Peter is identified as the disciple who cut off the ear of the high priest's servant, now named Malchus. Nothing is said about the disciples running away, but certainly they are absent as Jesus is tied and bound (John 18:12).

In John, Jesus and his disciples enter "into" (*eis*) the cultivated area, which implies that some kind of wall surrounded it. There was at least a clearly demarcated outside and inside. No details are given about the nature of the cultivation. That was not crucial to the story. Perhaps it was a small market garden. There is nothing said in any of the gospel accounts about the existence of a cave. Again, this was not necessary for the story.

Some very good reasons lead us to believe, however, that a cave was located in this walled, cultivated area, and that Jesus and his disciples slept in this cave rather than out in the open.

Looking closely at the text of John's gospel, we see that Jesus "went out" (*exēlthen*) of something within the garden to meet the soldiers (John 18:4). We know he did not go out of the garden enclosure itself, because the arrest is sited there: Later on, when Peter is questioned by witnesses, one of them says, "Didn't I see you in the garden (*kēpos*)?" (John 18:26).[2]

The Greek word *Gethsemane* comes from an Aramaic or Hebrew term that most likely means "oil press." The word *gat* on its own in Aramaic and Hebrew frequently refers to "wine press." But its meaning is actually broader. In rabbinic literature, *gat* refers to a place for the preparation of oil.[3] The broadest meaning of the word would encompass any pit or cave used for a particular purpose.[4] The Hebrew

INSIDE THE CAVE OF GETHSEMANE

Jesus and his disciples regularly spent the evenings on the Mount of Olives, and the warm, dry Cave of Gethsemane (shown in the photo and plan) would have been a natural place to find shelter. The cave's oil press would have operated only in the autumn and winter, after the olive harvest. By spring, when Jesus and his disciples came to Jerusalem to celebrate the festival of Passover, the cave would have been used only for storage. Thousands of people made pilgrimage to the Temple in Jerusalem during Passover, and every possible lodging in the city and surrounding village was offered to visitors.

Today, the cave is an underground chapel where services are held. The olive press may have been located in what is now the sanctuary (shown in the photo), in the easternmost extension of the cave. An ancient hole in the wall, visible through the square hole cut out of the modern wall just to the right of the altar, lies at the exact height to support the wooden beam of the press. The press would have extended out, parallel to the modern altar, in this eastern cave extension.

Few clues to the cave's original appearance remain. Star-shaped ceiling decorations and other rock paintings in the sanctuary date to the Crusader period (11th and 12th centuries); a recent mural behind the altar depicts Jesus and his disciples praying in the cave, with a large millstone beside them. The stone paving was laid after the excavations of 1956 and 1957, and the T-shaped concrete column at center is a modern support. Three ancient rock-cut pillars are covered with modern concrete.

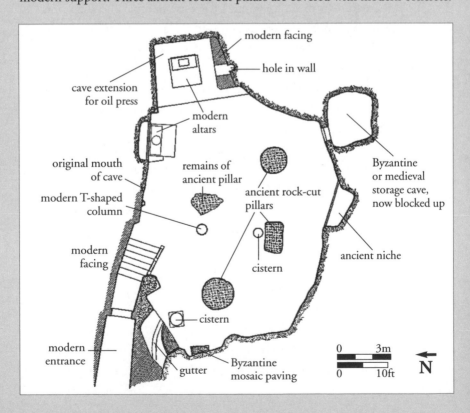

modern facing

hole in wall

cave extension
for oil press

modern
altars

original mouth
of cave

remains of
ancient pillar

ancient rock-cut
pillars

Byzantine
or medieval
storage cave,
now blocked up

modern T-shaped
column

modern
facing

ancient niche

cistern

cistern

modern
entrance

gutter

Byzantine
mosaic paving

0   3m

0   10ft

N

The remains of a fourth ancient pillar, to the right of the modern T-shaped column, are marked on the plan. The cave's original entrance was cut into the north wall. A gutter and Byzantine mosaics lie near the modern entrance.

The spacious cave, measuring 36 by 60 feet, was probably the largest olive-oil processing site on the Mount of Olives. The cave's central chamber was large enough to house a crushing basin with a millstone, used in the first step of olive pressing, although there are no archaeological remains.

word *shemanim*, a plural form, is used for different kinds of oil,[5] gifts of oil[6] and oil stores.[7] So we can assume the Hebrew name of the place was *Gat-Shemanim*, literally "press of oils." Since different grades of olive oil were made, the plural form may reflect the various distinctions or types.

The possible name of the cave in Aramaic, *Gatshemanin*, presumably sounded very much like Greek *Gethsēmani* (Mark 14:32) in the Aramaic Jerusalem dialect of the day. The final *t* of *gat* would have been pronounced as a soft *th*. In Greek the *sh* sounds of Aramaic and Hebrew were usually rendered simply by *sigma*, the Greek letter *s*. The *a* sound of *gat* seems to have been pronounced as an *e*, and the Aramaic plural ending *-in* seems to have lost its final letter in the local vocalization.

Archaeological evidence tends to support this cave as the site of Gethsemane. Excavations indicate that the present Gethsemane cave was indeed once used for pressing olive oil.[8]

The interior of the Gethsemane cave has greatly changed over the centuries and only vestiges of its original use remain (see plan, preceding pages). The present floor is about 40 inches above the level of the original floor. The cave is extremely large, measuring approximately 36 by 60 feet (11 by 18 meters). The cave roof was supported by four rock-cut pillars, three of which still exist. As noted above, the remains of the wide original entrance can be seen on the north side. An oil press probably stood in a roughly square artificial cave extension in the eastern wall. The evidence for this is a hole cut into the south wall of this recess. A hole in the wall may not seem like much proof, but it was most likely cut to hold the wooden horizontal bar of the press.[9] This beam held weights that created heavy pressure on the olives as the oil was being squeezed out. It is hard to imagine any other reason why someone would cut a hole in the wall here. We can be sure that the press was for olives and not for grapes, because wine presses are never found underground. Caves were often used for oil presses, however, because their warmth helped the process.[10]

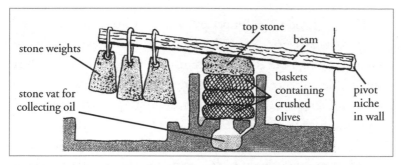

The beam olive press, used in the second step of olive pressing, extracted the last drops of oil from olives. First mill-stones crushed the olives in large basins to remove the finest, virgin oil used for sanctuary lamps. The remaining pulp was placed in loosely woven baskets (called aqalim *in Arabic and Hebrew) that were stacked on a smaller vat and topped with a stone. Pressure applied by the long wooden beam, anchored in the wall and weighted down with stones on one end, squeezed the remaining oil out of the pulp, through the baskets and into the stone vat below.*

The recent discovery of a number of olive-oil installations at ancient Maresha (Tell Sandahanna), in western Israel, provides useful information about olive presses in the centuries just before the time of Jesus. So does an olive-pressing installation in Jerusalem.[11]

The presses were located in caves. A beam was secured at one end between two rock-cut ledges in a deep recess in the cave wall, as was, no doubt, the beam of the Gethsemane press. Three stone weights were usually hung by a rope on the wooden beam. At Maresha, these stones weighed between 300 and 1,100 pounds.[12] A pit, into which the weights slowly descended, was cut in the floor. The mashed olives, stacked in baskets, were piled in a deep circular shaft between the rock ledges; the oil was collected in a vat below.

In eleven of the underground olive-pressing installations at Maresha, the presses were accompanied by circular crushing basins, almost 6.5 feet wide, with lens-shaped crushing stones. There are no remains of a crushing basin or stone in the Gethsemane cave today. In the ninth century, a monk named Bernard recorded that he saw four "round" or "curved" tables where Jesus and the apostles had supper.[13] This would fit well with the remnants of a circular crushing basin.

There is some reason to believe that the Gethsemane cave held not one, but two olive presses. The evidence for this appears in pilgrim accounts, dating from the sixth century to the Middle Ages, which testify to the existence of four rock ledges in the cave. Each recess for an olive press requires two rock ledges to support the press's beam. If the pilgrims saw four, then there may have been two presses. None of the pilgrims, however, suggests that the ledges have anything to do with olive pressing. Early in the sixth century, a pilgrim named Theodosius wrote that he saw four "couches" for the 12 apostles; he notes that "each couch holds three people."[14] The two ledges cut into recesses for the olive baskets and collecting vat in the press at Maresha measure about 40 inches wide by 40 inches high and are there wide enough for three (slim) people to sit on, side by side. It seems quite possible that Theodosius really saw the remains of two recesses for olive presses, with two ledges per recess.[15]

One of these ledges appears to have disintegrated by the end of the sixth century; an anonymous pilgrim from Piacenza, in about 570, mentions only three "couches."[16] Pilgrims wishing to take home mementos may have chipped the ledge away, or the rock may have simply fallen apart.[17] The pressure of the heavy beam on the oil baskets created lateral pressure on the rock into which the ledges were cut. Also, pilgrims would climb on these ledges to gain a spiritual reward. The Piacenza Pilgrim writes that he and his party reclined on the "couches" to gain their blessing. In time, if the rock was not strong, these ledges would have cracked.

The curved tables noted by Bernard in the ninth century also may have been remnants of the ledges, which had a concave arc cut out of them to fit around the baskets of olive pulp. With wear and tear and the edges chipped away, the ledges would have come to look much like facing semicircles. That only three ledges remained seems clear from a 12th-century pilgrimage account by Saewulf, who describes the three "beds" where the disciples Peter, James and John fell asleep.[18] Some time between the Middle Ages and today, these rocky ledges and the remains of the crushing basin were completely chipped away.

A pilgrim named Arculf reported to the abbot Adomnan of Iona
(c. 680) that he saw something else in the cave that we might associate with an olive-oil press. He spied a cistern "in the floor of the
cave ... [and] it has a huge shaft sunk deep, which goes down
straight." The remains of this cistern have been discovered below an
ancient hole in the cave ceiling, which was to let in air, light and
(periodically) rainwater. Adomnan tells us in fact that there were two
cisterns, one cut into the floor, and another that "goes down to an
untold depth below the mountain.[19]

That there were two cisterns in the ancient olive-pressing works is
not surprising. Water was useful for cleaning the olives and the equip-
ment, as well as for washing hands.

All this evidence leads to the conclusion that this cave was
clearly used for olive pressing and had a crushing basin near its
mouth, as well as two cisterns.

Even for an olive-oil press, the cave would have been unusually
large and impressive. As possibly the largest olive-oil processing site
on the Mount of Olives, it would have been well known.

The spacious cave would have been a useful storage area as well.
Oil presses were only used in the autumn and winter,[20] after the olive
harvest; by spring, when the festival of Passover took place, caves that
held olive presses were used only for storage. Therefore, when Jesus
and his disciples were in Jerusalem for Passover, the cave would not
have been used for oil pressing. However, it would have been an excel-
lent place to spend the night: warm, dry and roomy, with a cistern
inside for water. The owner of the property may have been sensible
enough to rent it out as accommodation. At festival times, thousands
of people came to Jerusalem,[21] and every lodging in the city and surrounding villages was taken. Any kind of shelter would have been considered as a lodging place. This cave was close to Jerusalem and probably securely located in a pleasant, cultivated enclosure.

It is extremely improbable that Jesus and his disciples would have
spent the night out in the open, sleeping amid olive trees. As anyone

knows who has camped in the Judean hills in spring, the nights are cold
and the dew is heavy. One simply cannot camp out without shelter at
this time of year without becoming extremely cold and damp. The
Gospel of John explicitly states that Jesus was arrested on a chilly night:
Peter stands warming himself by the fire in the courtyard of the high
priest "because it was cold" (John 18:18). The story of the young man
who was dressed only in a *sindōn* suggests that the disciples were pro-
tected from the weather. In the stuffy warmth of the cave, amid a slum-
bering mass of people, such attire would have been fine. But not out
in an olive grove in the freezing night!

That Jesus was arrested in or just outside a cave also fits well with
what we read in the gospel stories. We cannot know exactly what took
place in every detail because the Gospels differ, but the basic story
remains constant. It seems fairly clear that Jesus crossed over the
Kidron Valley (known here as the Valley of Jehoshaphat) with a group
of disciples and went a little way up the Mount of Olives to a cultivated
enclosure. The group went inside, as they often did. They had been
camping there for several days prior to the Passover festival. They either
rented the property, or else the owner offered it to them out of respect
for Jesus. We can imagine them entering the warm cave, lighting little
lamps and taking off their coats to sleep on as they prepared for bed.
Perhaps Jesus was restless and called Peter, James and John over, ask-
ing them to stay alert. He went forward from the cave entrance, still
within the cultivated enclosure but alone, praying in the darkness. In
the close coziness of the cave, and with heads befuddled with wine,
Peter, James and John fell asleep with everyone else. Jesus returned to
find them all blissfully unaware of what was about to happen. Then
Judas arrived with a group sent by the Roman and chief priestly
authorities of Jerusalem to arrest Jesus. Jesus came out of the cave
entrance and was greeted by Judas. The disciples awoke and realized
what was happening. A scuffle broke out. Some disciples tried to
defend Jesus; then, realizing it was hopeless, and perhaps admonished
by Jesus, they rapidly escaped. One young man lost his clothes in a

An Ancient Description of the Cave of Gethsemane

A seventh-century pilgrim named Arculf described the Cave of Gethsemane to a writer and abbot named Adomnan, who wrote the following report. Although the name Gethsemane is not used, it is clear that this is the cave referred to:

"Not far above the Church of Saint Mary on the Mount of Olives there is a cave which faces the Valley of Jehoshaphat. In it are two very deep wells: one goes down to an untold depth below the mountain, and the other is in the floor of the cave. It has a huge shaft sunk deep, which goes down straight. Over these wells there is a permanent covering. This cave also contains four rock tables. One of them, which is just inside the entrance, is that of the Lord Jesus, and sometimes his seat was certainly beside this small table, on the frequent occasions when he used to recline there and have a meal, and the twelve apostles reclined there with him at the other tables. The sealed mouth of the well which we described beneath the floor of the cave is to be seen closer to the tables of the apostles. According to what holy Arculf says, this cave has a small entrance which is closed by a wooden door, and he paid it many visits."

From Adomnan, *De Locis Sanctis* 15.1-3, trans. John Wilkinson in *Jerusalem Pilgrims Before the Crusades* (Warminster, England: Aris and Phillips, 1977).

struggle with a guard and then fled. Everyone ran away, and they were allowed to do so, for the authorities wanted only Jesus. They tied him up and marched him out to Jerusalem, leaving the cave of *Gat-Shemanin*, and the enclosed garden around it, empty.

Three hundred years later, Christians began to visit this cave to recall the arrest of Jesus, which they believed had taken place there. It was one of the earliest sites to be venerated by Christian pilgrims. Because the name of the place probably remained the same over the centuries, people had little difficulty in identifying it. The people of Jerusalem still spoke a dialect of Aramaic, now know as Syriac. The Jerusalem church may have kept alive the memory of the site of Jesus' betrayal. But, like the gospel writers before them, none of the earliest pilgrims mentions that Gethsemane was a cave, even though they are quite specific about its location.

The nun Egeria, for example, who made a famous tour of the Holy Land in about 382, describes the path followed by pilgrims on Good Friday. They go "into Gethsemane," where they are provided with candles "so that they can all see."[22] Clearly, they are going into some place that is darker than outside; but Egeria does not bother to note that it is a cave.

Only in the early-sixth-century account by Theodosius do we find explicit mention of Gethsemane as a large cave.[23] He writes: "This place is in a cave, and now two hundred monks go down there." But even after this date writers failed to note this feature.[24] Gethsemane was Gethsemane; somehow everyone knew it was a cave.

It was not until the 12th century that anyone thought of a Garden of Gethsemane, located adjacent to the cave. But the cave was never entirely abandoned even when Christian imagination, aided by the depictions of European art, sited the arrest in an olive grove. Western pilgrims began to associate the site with the place of Jesus' anxious prayer, called "the Agony." Eventually, even this identification became little known, but the cave remained a peculiar stop on the pilgrim trail—and remains so to this day—one that people often go into and out of without a second thought, presuming it to be nothing much, a mere invention. However, of all the traditional Christian holy sites in and around Jerusalem, the Cave of Gethsemane is one of the most likely to be authentic.

Since archaeology shows that the cave held an olive-oil press, and the Gospels refer to a place known as Gethsemane, which most likely meant "oil press," we are justified in considering the cave and Gethsemane to be one and the same. The cave is located just across the Kidron Valley, precisely where the Gospels suggest that Gethsemane was located. There is no other competing cave in the vicinity. Furthermore, Jesus and his disciples most likely did not lie down under the stars, but took shelter here during the cool spring nights. The evidence suggests that the cave of Gethsemane was the place they used as sleeping quarters, and here—or just outside—Judas caught them unawares.

1. For the authenticity of the story, see J.M. Ross, "The Young Man Who Fled Naked, Mark 14:51-2," *Irish Biblical Studies* 13:3 (1991), pp. 170-174. The beginning of the story differs slightly in Matthew and Mark. Matthew adds that Jesus stated directly that he wanted to "go away" to pray. Therefore, when it is written that he "took to himself" (*paralabōn*) Peter and the sons of Zebedee, it is not clear whether he had departed or was just about to. At any rate, the narrative makes it clear that the three apostles really stayed with the other disciples, for all of them together "forsook him and fled" (Matthew 26:56) when Jesus came back and was confronted by the arrest party.

2. For this observation, see Albert Storme, *Gethsemane* (Jerusalem: Franciscan Printing Press, 1972), p. 24.

3. Jerusalem Talmud, *Peah* 7:1; Tosephta, *Terumot* 3:6.

4. Compare Mishnah, *Zebahim* 14:1.

5. Babylonian Talmud, *Shabbat* 2:2.

6. Jerusalem Talmud, *Bezah* 1:9.

7. Babylonian Talmud, *Middot* 2:5.

8. See Virgilio Corbo, *Ricerche archeologiche al Monte degli Ulivi, Gerusalemme* (Jerusalem: Franciscan Printing Press, 1965), pp. 1-57; Louis-Hugues Vincent and Felix-M. Abel, *Jérusalem: recherches de topographie, d'archéologie et d'histoire. ii. Jérusalem nouvelle* (Paris: Gabalda, 1914), p. 335, fig. 147. See also, John Wilkinson, *Jerusalem as Jesus Knew It* (London: Thames and Hudson, 1978), pp. 127-131.

9. For olive presses in general, see Gustaf Dalman, *Arbeit und Sitte in Palästina* (Gütersloh, 1935), vol. 4, pp. 153-290. M. Heltzer and D. Eitam, eds., *Olive Oil in Antiquity: Papers of the Conference Held in Haifa* (Haifa: University of Haifa, 1987).

10. Dalman, *Arbeit and Sitte,* p. 322. There are many examples of underground oil presses from the region of Beth Guvrin. See Y. Teper, "The Oil Presses at Maresha Region," in *Olive Oil in Antiquity,* pp. 25-46, and Amos Kloner and Nahum Sagiv, "The Technology of Oil Production in the Hellenistic Period: Studies in the Crushing Process at Maresha," in *Olive Oil in Antiquity,* pp. 133-138.

11. I am indebted to Dr. Amos Kloner for this observation. I am also grateful to Dr. Kloner for taking me to visit some of these caves when I was annual scholar at the British School of Archaeology in 1986.

12. For further details, see Amos Kloner and Nahum Sagiv, "The Olive Presses of Hellenistic Maresha, Israel," in *Bulletin de Correspondence Héllenique Supplement* XXVI, pp. 119-135.

13. Bernard, *Itinerarium* 13.

14. Theodosius, *De Situ Terrae Sanctae* 10.

15. In my book, *Christians and the Holy Places: The Myth of Jewish-Christian Origins* (Oxford: Clarendon, 1993), p. 200, I suggested that these "ledges" may have been the remaining uprights of screw-operated presses. I am indebted to Dr. Kloner for pointing out that such screw presses only appeared at the end of the Roman period and were not in use at the time of Jesus.

16. Piacenza Pilgrim, *Itinerarium* 17.

17. In the Maresha cave, stone slabs, cut with concave arcs to fit snugly, were placed over the tops of ledges that had been cracked by extensive use. See Kloner and Sagiv, "Olive Presses," pp. 127-128.

18. Saewulf, *Relatio de peregrinatione* 17; compare Theoderic, *Liber de Locis Sanctis* 24, Second Guide 124.

19. Adomnan, *De Locis Sanctis* 1.15.1.

20. Dalman, *Arbeit und Sitte*, p. 322.

21. Josephus, *War* 7.1.9.

22. Egeria, *Itinerarium* 36.2.

23. Theodosius, *De Situ Terrae Sanctae* 10.

24. For details of these pilgrims, see *Christians and the Holy Places*, pp. 197-198.

CHAPTER THREE

WHAT REALLY HAPPENED AT GETHSEMANE?

Jerome Murphy-O'Connor

The scene has stimulated the imagination of great painters. The light of a full moon accentuates the shadows in a garden at the foot of the Mount of Olives. A lonely figure prays in anguish. Deep in careless sleep, his companions ignore his agony. The swords of the approaching soldiers appear on the horizon. The tension is palpable.

Jesus' prayer in the Gethsemane is one of the most soul-wrenching episodes in the Gospels: "My Father, if it is possible, let this cup pass from me. Yet, not as I will but as you (will)" (Matthew 26:39).

If the Transfiguration—the moment when Jesus is mystically transformed in the presence of Moses and Elijah—presents Jesus at his highest, here we see him at his lowest. The radiant Lord who stood erect on a mountain peak now struggles for light in the desolation of night. The disciples, who were so attentive at the Transfiguration and begged to prolong the golden moment, do not want to hear or see what is happening to Jesus here.

These contrasting images bear reflection. We like to bask in the glory of the superhuman Jesus of the Transfiguration. He is a savior to be proud of. We do not want to deal with a savior consumed by loneliness, desperate fear and uncertainty. These traits are far too human. Nonetheless, this is the real Jesus.

Jesus' struggle in Gethsemane is recounted in all three Synoptic Gospels (Matthew 26:36-46; Mark 14:32-42; and Luke 22:39-46). There are striking differences, however, which I want to explore here. As we shall see, one gospel actually contains two accounts of Jesus' agony.

What can we say of these varying accounts? Can we determine which was the most original and who copied from whom? Can we reconstruct how the story developed?

Luke's account (see box, p. 52) is much shorter than Mark's or Matthew's (see box, pp. 42-43). Mark and Matthew depict Jesus praying three times; Luke has only one prayer. The dominant scholarly hypothesis concerning the relationship between Matthew, Mark and Luke claims that when an episode is narrated by all three gospels, Mark, the earliest gospel, is the source; an episode found only in Matthew or Luke, on the other hand, goes back to a hypothetical source scholars call Q. Applying this two-source theory to the episode in Gethsemane, we find that Luke, with such a short account, must have severely abbreviated Mark. No other suggestion is seriously considered by scholars.[1]

Such radical surgery on the part of an evangelist would be most unusual, however. He might add or change, but not shorten so drastically. This suggests that the widely accepted two-source theory is not an appropriate framework in which to understand the Gethsemane episode. A very different solution becomes apparent if Mark and Matthew are first analyzed closely.

To help the reader do this, we have printed the text of Mark and Matthew side by side (see box, pp. 42-43). In the box on pages 46-47, we analyze a number of the most significant differences.[2]

The cumulative effect of the variations is to make it appear extremely likely that Matthew copied Mark's account, clarifying it and tidying it up with minor additions and omissions. Hence, if we are to discover what really happened in Gethsemane, we must focus on Mark.

Mark's account introduces us to doublets. Although to theatergoers the word *doublet* may evoke a tight-fitting jacket worn by men in 15th- and 16th-century Europe, to gospel scholars the term is much more mundane; it simply refers to a repeated element.

There are two types of doublets: verbal doublets, a saying or phrase that is repeated in a single gospel, and structural doublets, repeated elements that fulfill the same role in the framework or movement of the narrative.

Mark's account of Jesus in Gethsemane contains a whole series of structural doublets:

> The place to which Jesus and his disciples come is named twice: the Mount of Olives (14:26) and Gethsemane (14:34b).
>
> Twice Jesus gives an order to his disciples: "Sit here while I pray" (14:32b) and "Remain here and keep watching" (14:34b).
>
> The subjective state of Jesus is mentioned twice, first in indirect speech, "He began to be greatly distraught and troubled" (14:33a), and then in direct speech, "My soul is very sorrowful unto death" (14:34a).
>
> Similarly, the prayer of Jesus appears twice, again, first in indirect speech, "He was praying that if it is possible, the hour might pass from him" (14:35), and then in direct speech, "Abba, Father, all things are possible to you" (14:35), etc. This prayer is in fact a triplet, but note the vagueness of the third mention, "saying the same words" (14:39).
>
> The return of Jesus to his sleeping disciples is twice mentioned in virtually the same words: "He comes and finds them sleeping" (14:37), and "Having come, he found them sleeping" (14:40).
>
> Finally, the theme of handing over is evoked twice: "the Son of Man is given over into the hands of sinners" (14:41), and "the one who gives me over has come near" (14:42).

Such a consistent series of structural doublets permits only one conclusion: Mark's gospel combines two stories.

Jesus at Gethsemane: Two Versions

Close scrutiny of Matthew's and Mark's accounts of Jesus at Gethsemane reveals numerous correspondences as well as some tell-tale differences. As laid out here, passages that occur (sometimes word-for-word) in both gospels appear side-by-side. Where there is no close parallel, we've inserted a line space.

According to Mark (14:26,32-42)	According to Matthew (26:30,36-46)
26 And having sung a hymn, they went out to the Mount of Olives.	30 And having sung a hymn, they went out to the Mount of Olives.
32 And they come into the plot of land the name of which was Gethsemane; and he says to his disciples, "Sit here	36 Then Jesus comes with them into the plot of land called Gethsemane; and he says to his disciples, "Sit in this place until, going away,
while I pray."	I pray there."
33 And he takes along Peter, and James, and John with him, and he began to be greatly distraught and troubled.	37 And having taken along Peter and the two sons of Zebedee, he began to be sorrowful and troubled.
34 And he says to them, "My soul is very sorrowful unto death. Remain here and keep on watching."	38 Then he says to them, "My soul is very sorrowful unto death. Remain here and keep on watching with me."
35 And having gone forward a little, he was falling on the earth and was praying	39 And having gone forward a little, he was falling on his face praying and saying, "My Father,
that if it is possible the hour might pass from him.	if it is possible,
36 And he was saying, "Abba, Father, all things are possible to you. Take away this cup from me. But not what I will but what you (will)."	let this cup pass from me. Yet, not as I will but as you (will)."
37 And he comes and finds them sleeping, and he says to Peter, "Simon, are you sleeping? Were you not strong enough to watch one hour?	40 And he comes to the disciples and finds them sleeping, and he says to Peter, "So ye were not strong enough to watch one hour with me!

Mark (continued)

38 Keep ye watching and praying lest ye
enter into trial. Indeed the spirit is
willing, but the flesh is weak."
39 And again having gone away, he
he prayed, saying
the same word.

40 And again having come,
he found them sleeping; for
their eyes were very burdened,
and they did not know what they
should answer him.

41 And he comes the third time, and
says to them, "Do you go on
sleeping, then, and taking your rest?
The money is paid.
The hour has come.
Behold the Son of Man is given over
into the hands of sinners.
42 Get up; let us go! Behold
the one who gives me over
has come near."

Matthew (continued)

41 Keep ye watching and praying lest ye
enter into trial. Indeed the spirit is
willing, but the flesh is weak."
42 Again, a second time, having gone
away, he prayed, saying,

"My Father, if it is not possible for
this to pass, let your will be done."
43 And having come,
again he found them sleeping; for
their eyes were burdened.

44 And having left them, again having
gone away, he prayed a third time,
saying the same word again.
45 Then he comes to the disciples, and
says to them, "Do you go on
sleeping, then, and taking your rest?

Behold the hour has come near,
And the Son of Man is given over
into the hands of sinners.
46 Get up; let us go! Behold,

there has come near
the one who gives me over."

Can they be reconstructed? Several scholars have answered yes.[3]

At least one leading New Testament scholar, the late Raymond Brown, dismissed the whole effort however: "The theory smacks somewhat of the way modern scholars would work, combining lines from two books propped up on either side of them."[4] In Brown's view, the variety of proposed solutions betrayed the futility of the enterprise. In fact, these successive attempts to account for the doublets indicate that scholars of different backgrounds have recognized a real problem that escaped Brown.

Two aspects of Brown's criticism, however, are not entirely off target. First, scholars have at times permitted idiosyncratic judgments to influence their reconstructions. More importantly, as Brown pointed out, none of the proposed reconstructions takes into consideration the order of the doublets. The implication is that a reconstruction that does follow the order of the doublets would be taken seriously, even by Brown. Such a reconstruction is precisely what I propose (see box, pp. 52-53).

The interlocking stories slide apart without difficulty. Each of the sources combined in Mark is a complete story containing but one prayer of Jesus. When combined, this became two prayers, which Mark increased to three by adding, "And again having gone away, he prayed, saying the same words" (14:39), which entailed the insertion of "again" in 14:40 and "He comes the third time" in 14:41. The lack of any content for the third prayer betrays that Mark was interested primarily in the number three, although his reasoning can only be a matter of speculation. One possibility, as Brown suggested, is that the triple failure of the disciples to stay awake was intended to balance the triple denial by Peter (Mark 14:66-72).[5]

Having identified Mark's two sources, the next question is whether we can determine their relative antiquity. Is Source A older than Source B, or the reverse? Several hints suggest that Source A is older.

First, as stories are retold, they often become more specific as ambiguities pointed out by the audience are clarified. This appears to have happened in Mark.

Source A, for example, mentions "the Mount of Olives" (14:26b) and "his disciples" (14:32b). These give rise to the obvious questions: Precisely where on the Mount of Olives, which is quite a large area? And which disciples? Both of these questions are answered by Source B, which locates the episode in "a plot of land called Gethsemane" (14:32a) and names the key disciples as "Peter and James and John" (14:33a). Source B, therefore, is more developed than Source A.

Second, as a general rule, stories that focus on Jesus while leaving the disciples in the background are older than stories that emphasize the disciples' presence. The earliest stories were told by eyewitnesses who knew what they had seen. The second generation of Christians, on the other hand, had to rely on what they were told; they needed to be reassured that those who told the story knew what they were talking about. Consequently, later stories tend to stress that first-generation disciples *were* present and involved and therefore were able to report accurately.

Thus, in Source A, Jesus separates himself from his disciples. He tells them, "Sit here while I pray" (14:32b) and moves away (14:35a). In Source B, however, Jesus exhorts his disciples to "keep watching" (14:34b).[6] Jesus' movement away is not mentioned explicitly in Source B. Rather, his departure has to be inferred from his return to the disciples in 14:37. The need for Jesus to be observed is apparent in Source B although it was frustrated by the sleep of the disciples. The editor's respect for his source did not permit him to pretend that the disciples remained awake, but he used their slumber for a little moral lesson, "Watch and pray lest ye enter into trial" (14:38), which deflects attention from Jesus to the needs of the early Church. On this basis, too, Source A appears to be earlier.

Let us look more closely now at the contents of Source A. It is perfectly plausible that Jesus and his disciples should head for the Mount of Olives after an evening meal in Jerusalem. They were poor Galileans who could not afford to lodge in a city crowded with wealthier pilgrims. The resident population of Jerusalem at that time has

WHICH CAME FIRST?

Did Matthew copy Mark or the other way around? Clearly the accounts in both gospels are closely related. In many places, they are identical. One must have copied from the other. To determine which came first, we must look closely at the significant differences. In each case we must ask which author created the difference by adding or subtracting from his source. This involves weighing probabilities. Certainty may elude us. This might seem a fragile basis on which to reconstruct the life of Jesus, but it is just the sort of judgment we make all the time in ordering our lives.

Sometimes the judgment is not too difficult. Compare Mark 14:32 with Matthew 26:36, the introduction to the story. Mark says, "they come." Matthew says, "Jesus comes with them." Mark is vague. One has to know that "they" includes Jesus, who is never explicitly mentioned.

In the same verses, Mark has Jesus saying to his disciples, "Sit here," while Matthew has, "Sit in this place." The word "here" in Mark is somewhat confusing because it gives the impression that Jesus was to stay close to the disciples, whereas in the next verse he moves away. In Matthew, the disciples are told to "sit in this place until, going away, I will pray there."

Both the vagueness of "they come" and the slight confusion caused by "sit here" in Mark's account are rectified in Matthew. Here Jesus is mentioned by name, and Jesus' move away is announced.

Did Matthew solve a problem by changing Mark, or did Mark create a problem by changing Matthew? The choice is an easy one. Matthew was smoothing out Mark.

Now let's compare Mark 14:33 with Matthew 26:37, where Jesus' subjective state is described. Mark says he is "distraught and troubled"; Matthew says "sorrowful and troubled." It is more likely that Matthew changed "distraught" to "sorrowful" to conform with what Jesus says of himself, "My soul is very sorrowful."

The next comparison involves what happens to Jesus. In Mark, Jesus collapses, "falling on the earth" (14:35) in an uncontrolled reaction to severe stress. In Matthew, Jesus is "falling on his face" (26:39). This is the classic Jewish posture of prayer, as in Genesis 17:3: "Abram fell on his face" (see also Judges 13:20). Again, our choice is easy. It is most improbable that Mark would defame Jesus by transforming the controlled gesture (prayer) of an entirely self-possessed person into an uncontrolled reaction (despair), whereas it is very likely that Matthew would attempt to improve the image of Jesus by substituting a controlled reaction for an uncontrolled one.

Now let's look at Jesus' prayer. Matthew's version (26:39) is much shorter than Mark's (14:35-36). Our first reaction might be that Mark had expanded on Matthew.[1] Yet if we look closely at Mark, we immediately notice two internal contradictions. First, Jesus prays that "if it is possible the hour might pass" (Mark 14:35). This "if" contrasts with the certitude in the next verse, in which Jesus says, "All things are possible ... Take away this cup" (Mark 14:36). Second, in these two verses the object of Jesus' prayer shifts from "the hour" to "this cup." These contradictions in Mark are eliminated by Matthew: "If it is possible, let this cup pass from me" (Matthew 26:39). This simplification then enables Matthew to create a second prayer, in 26:42, which has no parallel in Mark 14:39.

Matthew's version of events at Gethsemane includes not only two prayers, but also a reference, in 26:44, to a third prayer, in which Jesus says "the same word." The first two prayers of Jesus in Matthew exhibit Jesus' increasing degree of acceptance of his Father's will. In the first (26:39) Jesus still thinks he might be allowed to escape his fate ("If it is possible ... "), but nonetheless submits to his Father's will. In the second prayer (36:42), this hope has been abandoned ("If it is not possible ..."); his submission is complete. If Mark had had this text before him, he would not have changed it.

Mark 14:37 also might have caused some confusion for an early audience. In this passage, Jesus says to Peter, "Simon, are you sleeping?" Only someone familiar with the Gospels would know that Simon and Peter were one and the same person ("He gave the name Peter to Simon" [Mark 3:16]). This minor difficulty is compounded by the pointlessness of his question. We have just been told that Jesus found all the disciples sleeping (Mark 14:37).

As we would expect, Matthew takes care of these difficulties, this time by omitting both the name Simon and the pointless question (Matthew 26:40).[2]

In Mark 14:40, we are told that Jesus found the disciples sleeping. This is immediately followed with the somewhat incongruous statement that "they did not know what they should answer him." If the disciples were asleep, how did they know that Jesus had returned? And why would they reply when Jesus had said nothing?[3] And why would they be troubled over what to answer when they were asleep? Matthew wisely omitted "and they did not know what to answer him."

Mark 14:41 contains an enigmatic and seemingly meaningless statement without context: "The money is paid" (*apechei*, in Greek). Scholars fiercely dispute the meaning of this Greek word. Matthew omits it, doubtless because he could not understand it either.[4]

A final bit of confusion or tension appears in Mark 14:41, in which Jesus says that "the hour has come," implying that his arrest is imminent. In the next verse, however, Jesus says that "the one who gives me over [Judas]" has not yet arrived; he has only "come near." Matthew solves this problem by using the same verb, "to come near," both of the hour and of Judas (Matthew 26:45-46).—J.M.-O.

---

1. Matthew does expand Luke in the case of the Lord's Prayer (compare Matthew 6:9-13 and Luke 11:24).

2. In addition, Matthew did not tolerate the tension between the singular "Were you not strong enough to watch one hour?" and the plural "Keep ye watching" (Mark 14:38), so he has Jesus accuse all the disciples (Matthew 26:40).

3. In Mark there is no departure corresponding to the third return in Mark 14:41. Had there been one in his source, why would Mark have omitted it? Hence, it is Matthew who added the departure (26:44) for the sake of neatness, and moved up the ordinal "third" to match "a second time," which he had inserted in 26:42 to make the numerical series complete.

4. Raymond E. Brown, *The Death of the Messiah: From Gethsemane to the Grave*, Anchor Bible Reference Library (New York: Doubleday, 1994), p. 1379.

been estimated at between 40,000[7] and 60,000.[8] During pilgrimage feasts, the population swelled to about 180,000.[9] Space in the city, therefore, was at a premium.

The close relationship between Jesus and the family of Martha, Mary and Lazarus, who lived in the village of Bethany (John 11:1-3), suggests that Jesus made his base with them when he came to Jerusalem.[10] It was only 2 miles from the city (John 11:18). Jesus had to climb the Mount of Olives each day to reach the city and again on his return at night (Mark 11:11-12). On the night of the Agony, Jesus and his disciples were returning to Bethany on the eastern slope of the Mount of Olives: "And every day he was teaching in the Temple, but at night he went out and lodged on the Mount of Olives" (Luke 21:37).

The traditional site of Gethsemane has much to recommend its authenticity. When the church historian and bishop Eusebius of Caesara wrote his *Onomasticon* (an alphabetic list of biblical places with descriptions of their history and geography) at some point between 324 and 336, Gethsemane was already a well-established place of prayer, on the basis of a tradition transmitted by the Christian community of Jerusalem, which had never abandoned the city.[11] The site now marked by the Church of All Nations is in fact located at the easiest point to start climbing up the Mount of Olives. Today three roads radiate upwards from that point and come together on the ridge that leads to Bethany. The path that Jesus and his disciples intended to follow is undoubtedly that marked by an ancient flight of rock-cut steps, which may still be seen in the garden of the Russian Church of Saint Mary Magdelene,[12] just upslope from the Church of All Nations.

On reaching the Mount of Olives, Source A tells us, Jesus "began to be deeply distraught and troubled" (14:33b). Exegetes have struggled to find adequate words to bring out the force of the two Greek verbs used here, *ekthambeô* and *adêmoneô*.

Ekthambeô is often translated "amazed," but the connotations of "amazement" in current English (entertained, amused) make it inappropriate. The context here demands the element of shock that the verb carries in Mark 10:24 and 16:5-6. It is a matter of "terrified surprise,"[13] a dawning awareness that produces "shuddering horror."[14]

The usual translation of *adêmoneô* is "to be distressed, troubled," but the connotations of the verb as established by usage go much further. One commentator has noted that the term "describes the confused, restless, half-distracted state, which is produced by physical derangement or by mental distress ... [T]he primary idea of the word will be loathing and discontent."[15]

In short, Jesus began to be filled with appalling dread.

The only explanation of this paroxysm of instinctive revulsion is that Jesus had become aware that his death was imminent. But why was the impact so great at this point? I am convinced that he had already come to terms with his death, realizing that his death would be *the* saving event in God's plan for humanity.[16] After all, Jesus had previously foreseen and predicted his death (Mark 8:31, 9:31, 10:33-34). Something must have happened in Mark 14:33 to bring his awareness of his death to a different level. What provoked the shocking shift from the theoretical to the real—a shift that almost broke Jesus?

The most probable answer lies in the setting. Jesus reached the foot of the Mount of Olives by the Kidron Valley (John 18:1). Today both sides of the valley are lined with tombs, Muslim on the west and Jewish on the east, because both religions believe the valley to be the place of the Last Judgment. By Jesus' time what is now the village of Silwan was a great graveyard.[17] Between it and Gethsemane, two huge tomb monuments (the so-called tombs of Absalom and Zechariah) marked catacombs cut into the cliff.[18] They would have been perfectly visible in the full moon of Passover. Jesus had been under direct threat since Caiaphas had decreed that "one man should die for the people" (John 11:50). Weighed down with apprehension, the sight of the tombs lining his route forced the thought of death from his head to his heart. He became profoundly disturbed at the thought, "It might be tonight!"

Jesus manages to control himself sufficiently to tell his disciples to wait while he struggles for self-mastery in prayer. Then, overwhelmed by the hidden fears surging over him, he collapses on the ground.[19] Does he pray? "If it is possible"—Jesus' words in Mark 14:35b—suggest he is not even sure that God can help him. His is almost a cry of despair over the nearness of the "hour" of his destiny. The prayer is followed by silence. God has not answered.

Somehow Jesus finds the internal strength to pull himself together. He accepts his destiny while his weary disciples sleep. His questions mock their self-absorption.

If the disciples were asleep, how did they know what was happening to Jesus?[20] In other words, where did the information in Source A come from? It is difficult to imagine that it came from Jesus himself. He was arrested immediately afterwards, and there is no hint that he had any opportunity to speak to his disciples before he was put to death. Even if he had, they probably would have talked of other matters.

If Jesus was not the source, then the only possibility is that certain disciples projected onto Jesus the emotions that they imagined they would experience if they suddenly realized their death was imminent.[21] As the followers of a crucified criminal, they knew that they were walking a dangerous path and must have reflected frequently on how *they* would react if threatened with death. The disciples who composed Source A were honest with themselves. They did not flatter themselves about their courage in a crisis. They understood that mastery of the deep-rooted instinct of self-preservation would not come easily and they presumed that Jesus felt the same way. They fully accepted his humanity. He was like them in all things except sin (Hebrews 2:17, 4:15). They did not imagine Jesus as a superman, with no fears or frailties.

The intensely human Jesus revealed by Source A—a leader on the verge of a nervous breakdown—proved to be more than some other Christians could accept. In consequence, they wrote a different version of what happened in Gethsemane. Their version has survived as Source B.

Source B lacks the explicit statement that Jesus "became filled with terrified surprise and distressed from shock" (Mark 14:33b).[22] Instead, in Source B Jesus speaks for himself: "My soul is very sorrowful unto death" (Mark 14:34a). On the surface this appears to convey the same emotional state.[23] In fact, ancient readers (or listeners) would have recognized the allusions to Psalm 42:6,12, "Why are you very sorrowful, my soul, and why do you distress me?" and, perhaps, to Jonah 4:9, "I am so weighed down by sorrow, I want to die." In Source B Jesus is sufficiently composed to make scriptural allusions.

This is a radical change from the mood of Source A. The man in intense agony has become calm enough to quote scripture. The individual suffering a private hell has been replaced by a familiar religious type, either the just man of the Psalms, who suffers persecution yet is sustained by God,[24] or the weary prophet, who begs for release by death.[25]

Jesus' prayer in Source B (Mark 14:36) contains no hint of the anguished doubt so vivid in Source A (Mark 14:35). In Source B, Jesus, addressing God with the utmost formality as "Abba, Father," replaces doubt with certitude: "All things are possible to you."[26]

The final element in Jesus' prayer in Source B is, "But not what I will but what you (will)" (Mark 14:36). Nothing remotely resembling this petition appears in Source A. It is the perfect submission to the will of God that is expected of all Christians. Such concentration on the way believers should live has taken us a long way from the stark struggle of Source A. The Jesus of Source B is calm and collected, introducing scriptural allusions to stimulate the theological reflection of his disciples and offering them an example and advice for the living of their Christian lives.

Mark must have been aware of how different the two Gethsemane stories were. Why then did he combine his two sources rather than choose between them? The simplest answer is that he was not willing to throw away a scrap of the tradition about Jesus. He could see no justification for preserving Source B at the expense of Source A, or vice versa. Human nature being what it is, one might suspect that Mark personally preferred Source B, but he also knew his audience and recognized that, when combined, Source A would be interpreted in the light of Source B.

THE SOURCES OF INSPIRATION

The repetitions in Mark's account of the Agony suggest to author Jerome Murphy-O'Connor that Mark was working from two earlier sources, referred to here as A and B. Mark apparently felt that he should not omit anything found in his sources, and thus combined them. Luke, too, had access to Sources A and B and tried to be faithful to them, but he strove to avoid repetition. That is one reason why his account is so much shorter than Mark's.

Sources A and B are reconstituted in full at right. The phrases and ideas Luke borrowed from these sources appear in italics. Brackets [ ] indicate where Mark's gospel contains material not found in Sources A and B.

As Luke wove together passages from Sources A and B, he sometimes altered the phrasing and the order. So that you can see precisely what changes Luke made, in the right column on the facing page we've isolated the passages that Luke adapted from Sources A and B and aligned them, side-by-side, with the originals (in italics in the left column).

Below, we see Luke's full gospel account of the Agony, with the material he borrowed from A and B in italics.

Luke's Finished Account
Luke 22:39-46

39And having gone out, he proceeded according to his custom *to the Mount of Olives*; and *the disciples* too followed him. 40And being at the place, he said to them, "*Keep on praying not to enter into trial.*" 41And *he drew away from them as if a stone's throw*; and having knelt he was praying, 42saying, "*Father, if you desire, take away this cup from me. Nevertheless, not my will but yours be done.*" 43But an angel from heaven appeared to him, strengthening him. 44And *being in agony*, he was praying more earnestly. And *his sweat became as if drops of blood falling down to the earth.* 45And having stood up from prayer, having come to the disciples, *he found them asleep for sorrow*; 46and he said to them." *Why do you sleep? Having stood up, keep on praying lest you enter into trial.*"

The Sources of Mark and Luke (derived from Mark 14:26,32-42)	What Luke Took from the Sources

Source A

26 They went out *to the Mount of Olives.*

32b And he says to *his disciples,*
"Sit here while I pray."

33b And *he began to be greatly distraught and troubled.*

35 And *having gone forward a little,* he was falling on the earth, and was praying that *if it is possible,* the hour might pass from him.

40 Having come [ ],
*he found them sleeping,
for their eyes were very burdened.*

41 [ ] And he says to them,
"*Do you go on sleeping,*
then, and taking your rest? The money is paid. The hour has come. [ ]

42 *Get up*; let us go. Behold the one who gives me over has come near."

Luke's Use of Source A

39a *to the Mount of Olives*
39b *the disciples*

44 *Being in agony ... his sweat became as if drops of blood falling down to the earth*
41 *he drew away from them as if a stone's throw*
42b *if you desire*

45 *he found them asleep for sorrow*

46 *Why do you sleep?*

46b *having stood up*

Source B

32a They come to the plot of land the name of which was Gethsemane.

33a And he takes along Peter, and James, and John with him. 34And he says to them, "My soul is very sorrowful unto death. Remain here and keep watching."

36 And he was saying, "Abba, *Father,* all things are possible to you. *Take away this cup from me. But not what I will but what you (will).*"

37 And he comes and finds them sleeping, and he says to Peter, "Simon, are you sleeping? Were you not strong enough to watch one hour?

38 *Keep ye watching and praying lest ye enter into trial.* Indeed the spirit is willing but the flesh is weak."

40b And they did not know what they should answer him.

Luke's Use of Source B

42a *Father*

42c *Take away this cup from me*
42d *Nevertheless, not my will but yours be done*

40 *Keep on praying not to enter into trial*
46 *Keep on praying lest ye enter into trial*

Having examined both of Mark's sources, we are now in a position to appreciate Luke's shorter narrative, which resembles Sources A and B individually to the extent that each has only one prayer of Jesus, as opposed to the three prayers in the final versions of both Mark and Matthew.

Luke's text is an extraordinary combination of elements that reflect different parts of Source A and Source B of Mark (see box, pp. 52-53). It would appear that Luke tried to be faithful to both sources, but without combining them as Mark did.

Luke's version also contains two distinctive elements: Jesus' blood-like sweat (Luke 22:44) and the angel (Luke 22:43). Some scholars argue that these elements were added a century or so after Luke's gospel was composed. This is not the place to debate this highly technical problem, but I am inclined to agree with Brown that on balance the evidence favors the view that they always belonged to the gospel.[27]

A sweat of blood is not physically impossible.[28] Luke, however, does not speak of a sweat of blood but of a sweat so profuse that it was *like* blood. The cause of this sweat was Jesus' "agony." To us this suggests intense suffering, but to a first-century reader it would have evoked a struggle for victory.[29] Luke mentions the drenching perspiration to underline the intense internal struggle that demanded every ounce of Jesus' concentration and energy.

Where Mark's Source A presents a Jesus who is "deeply distraught and troubled," Luke, with his refined sense of graphic artistry, is much less explicit, simply referring to bloodlike sweat. And Luke betrays his preference for Source B by introducing the angel before mentioning the bloodlike sweat. Someone interested only in telling the story would have used the natural order of problem ("the agony") followed by solution (the appearance of the angel). By mentioning the angel first, Luke ensured that his readers would not take Jesus' "agony" too seriously. After all, what could possibly happen to Jesus when a powerful heavenly figure was there to comfort and fortify him?

Further evidence for Luke's preference for the perspective of Source B is provided by Jesus' posture as he prays. As we have noted, in Mark 14:35 Jesus collapses; in Matthew 26:39 Jesus assumes the classic Jewish position of reverence, with his face to the ground. Luke, for his part, has Jesus "drop to his knees," a totally controlled posture that had become the standard for Christian prayer when Luke wrote.[30]

The angel in Luke's version softens God's silence in Source A and God's refusal to answer Jesus' prayer in Source B. The divine response in Luke is still negative, but God relents to the extent of strengthening Jesus to drink the cup of suffering: "An angel from heaven appeared to him, strengthening him" (Luke 22:43).

Reading the accounts in the probable order of composition, we see Jesus' acceptance of his fate becoming progressively more perfect. The culmination of this process is to be found in John's version.

John usually does not repeat events that have been adequately described by the other evangelists, but evokes them in a different context by means of a highly specific allusion.[31] That is the case here. John anticipates Jesus' prayer in Gethsemane: "Now is my soul distressed, and what shall I say, 'Father, save me from this hour? No, for this purpose I have come to this hour. Father, glorify your name!' Then a voice came from heaven, 'I have glorified it, and I will glorify it again!' The crowd standing by heard it and said that it had thundered. Others said, 'An angel had spoken to him'" (John 12:27-29).

The connection of this passage with the Gethsemane episode in the other Gospels is clear:[32] "My soul is distressed" evokes Psalm 42:6,12 in exactly the same way as Mark's "My soul is very sorrowful" (Mark 14:34a); a petition concerning "the hour" resembles Mark's "if it is possible 'the hour' might pass from him" (Mark 14:35); and the angel appears in Luke's account (Luke 22:43).

In John's gospel, Jesus' submission to the will of his Father is so perfect that he will not even ask for deliverance. He refuses to utter the prayer attributed to him by Matthew, Mark and Luke. Jesus explicitly acknowledges that throughout his ministry the divine will has guided him to this moment. Why should he at the last minute refuse the whole purpose of his life? On the contrary, he glorifies the Father, and this time there is a positive response from heaven: "I have glorified it, and will glorify it again" (John 12:28). With this reference to a past moment of glorification, John evokes the Transfiguration, which he does not describe explicitly elsewhere.[33]

With John we have come very far from the lonely figure in the moonlight-dappled garden, whose body and spirit momentarily rebelled against what he knew to be the inexorable plan of his Father for the salvation of humanity.

1. Thus, for example, Joseph A. Fitzmyer, *The Gospel According to Luke*, Anchor Bible series 28A (Garden City, NY: Doubleday, 1985), p. 1438.

2. To bring out even the most minute differences between the Gospels, a very literal translation has been used. It is taken from Raymond E. Brown, *The Death of the Messiah: From Gethsemane to the Grave*, Anchor Bible Reference Library (New York: Doubleday, 1994), pp. 1583-1602.

3. Their proposals are listed below. Elements added by Mark when he combined the two sources are not taken into account.

For Source A, Rudolf Thiel (*Drei Markus-Evangelien* [Berlin: De Gruyter, 1938], p. 23) includes 14:33,34,35a,36,37,38; Emanuel Hirsch (*Die Frühgeschichte des Evangeliums, I. Das Werden des Markus-Evangeliums* [Tübingen: Vandenhoeck & Ruprecht, 1951], pp. 156-157), 14:34,35,37,42; Karl Georg Kuhn ("Jesus in Gethsemane," *Evangelische Theologie* 12 [1951-1952], pp. 266-267), 14:32,35,40,41; Pierre Benoit ("Les outrages à Jésus Prophète," in *Neotestamentica et Patristica*, Festschrift for O. Cullmann [Leiden: Brill, 1962], p. 103 n. 8), 14:32a,34b, 32b,35,[40-41a],41b,42; Marie-Emile Boismard (*Synopse des Quatres Evangiles en Français II* [Paris: Cerf, 1972], pp. 392-393), 14:26,32b,35a,36,40,41; J. Warren Holleran (*The Synoptic Gethsemane, Analecta Gregoriana* 191 [Rome: Gregorian University, 1973], p. 144), 14:32,33b,35,40,41,42a; Xavier Léon-Dufour ("Jésus à Géthsamani: Essai de lecture synchronique," *Science et esprit* 31 [1979], p. 251), 14:32,33b,35,40,50; David Stanley (*Jesus in Gethsemane: The Early Church Reflects on the Suffering of Jesus* [New York: Paulist, 1980], pp. 108-111), 14:32,33b,35,40,41, 42a.

For Source B, Thiel includes 14:32,39,35b,40,41a; Hirsch, 14:32,36,38a,41; Kuhn 14:33,34,36,37,38; Benoit, 14:33,34ac,39,36,37,38; Boismard, 14:32a,33, 34b,38,39,36,37; Holleran, 14:33a,34,39a,36,37,38; Léon-Dufour, 14:33a,34, 36,37; Stanley, 14:26b,33a,34,36,37,38.

4. Brown, *Death of the Messiah*, p. 221.

5. Brown, *Death of the Messiah*, p. 204.

6. This tendency is accentuated by Matthew's addition, "keep watching with me" (v. 38).

7. Magen Broshi, "La population de l'ancienne Jérusalem," *Revue biblique* 82 (1975), p. 13. He bases his estimate on the average number of inhabitants per acre, in contrast to Wilkinson (see next note), who bases his estimate on the city's water supply.

8. John Wilkinson, "Ancient Jerusalem—Its Water Supply and Population," *Palestine Exploration Quarterly* 106 (1974), p. 49.

9. See Joachim Jeremias, *Jerusalem in the Time of Jesus—An Investigation into Economic and Social Conditions During the New Testament Period* (London: SCM, 1969), p. 84. Jeremias bases his estimate on an average of 18,000 sacrificial lambs multiplied by an average of 10 at each meal (p. 83).

10. See Sylvester Saller, *Excavations at Bethany (1949-53)* (Jerusalem: Franciscan Press, 1957).

11. See Jerome Murphy-O'Connor, "Pre-Constantinian Christian Jerusalem," in Anthony O'Mahony, Göran Gunner, Kevork Hintlian, eds., *The Christian Heritage in the Holy Land* (London: Scorpion Cavendish, 1995), pp. 15-17.

12. Louis-Hugues Vincent and Felix-Marie Abel, *Jérusalem nouvelle* (Paris: Gabalda, 1914), p. 305.

13. Henry Barclay Swete, *The Gospel According to St. Mark* (London: Macmillan, 1908), p. 342.

14. Brown, *Death of the Messiah*, p. 153.

15. Joseph Barber Lightfoot, *Saint Paul's Epistle to the Philippians* (London: Macmillan, 1908), p. 123.

16. See Murphy-O'Connor, "What Really Happened at the Transfiguration?" *Bible Review*, Fall 1987, p. 18.

17. David Ussishkin, *The Village of Silwan* (Jerusalem: Israel Exploration Society and Yad Izhak Ben-Zvi, 1993).

18. For description and dating, see Kay Prag, *Jerusalem*, Blue Guide (London: Black, 1989), pp. 247-251.

19. So, rightly, David Stanley, *Jesus in Gethsemane*, p. 134. Brown reluctantly concedes that Jesus' action complements what is said of his distraught state, but then says that Matthew "slightly softens Mark's picture of Jesus' distress" (*Death of the Messiah*, p. 165). In fact, Matthew changes the picture completely (as does Luke) by substituting a controlled action for an uncontrolled one.

20. The question is raised by Stanley (*Jesus in Gethsemane*, p. 140) but not really answered.

21. Brown says that "there was an early Christian memory or understanding that Jesus struggled with and prayed to God about his impending death" (*Death of the Messiah*, p. 177, cf. p. 225), but does not say where either came from. When he wrote his commentary on John 12:27-28, Brown suggested, "Since there were no witnesses to report the prayer of Jesus during the agony (the disciples were asleep at a distance), the tendency would be to fill in the skeletal framework of the Gethsemane scene with prayers and sayings uttered by Jesus at other times" (*The Gospel According to John [I-XIII]*, Anchor Bible series 29 [Garden City, NY: Doubleday, 1966], p. 471).

22. Stanley's translation (*Jesus in Gethsemane*, p. 108).

23. It is paraphrased "My sorrow is so great that it almost overwhelms me" in Christopher S. Mann, *Mark*, Anchor Bible series 27 (New York: Doubleday, 1986), p. 587.

24. J. Warren Halloran, *The Synoptic Gethsemane, Analecta Gregoriana* 191 (Rome: Gregorian University, 1973), p. 207.

25. David Daube, "Death as a Release in the Bible," *Novum Testamentum* 5 (1962), pp. 96-98. This study also evokes Moses (Numbers 11:15), Elijah (1 Kings 19:4) and Jeremiah (Jeremiah 20:14-18).

26. Cf. Mark 10:27.

27. Brown, *Death of the Messiah*, pp. 180-186.

28. Brown cites medical evidence of "instances of hematidrosis, involving intense dilation of subcutaneous capillaries that burst into the sweat glands. The blood then clots and is carried to the surface of the skin by the sweat" (*Death of the Messiah*, pp. 185).

29. "But it is also well attested for a state of mind associated with fear or anguish because of some impending, uncertain experience or phenomenon" (Fitzmyer, *The Gospel According to Luke*, p. 1444).

30. Precisely these words are used of the prayers of Peter (Acts 9:40), Paul (Acts 20:36) and the community at Tyre (Acts 21:5). Kneeling while praying was not unknown among the Jews; see 1 Kings 8:54 (which, however, contradicts 1 Kings 8:22!) and Daniel 6:10.

31. For example, John's version of the Last Supper (John 13:1-20) does not contain the institution of the Eucharist (Mark 14:22-25 = Matthew 26:26-29 = Luke 22:15-20), but in the discourse on the bread of life (John 6:26-59), which takes place much earlier in the ministry of Jesus, John evokes the Eucharist by the words, "The bread which I shall give for the life of the world is my flesh ... [U]nless you eat the flesh of the Son of Man and drink his blood, you have no life in you; he who eats my flesh and drinks my blood has eternal life" (John 6:51-54).

32. Brown, *The Gospel According to John*, p. 470.

33. Brown, *The Gospel According to John*, p. 476.

CHAPTER FOUR

JESUS' TRIUMPHAL MARCH TO THE CRUCIFIXION

Thomas Schmidt

Scholars have long recognized that the evangelists do not simply report on the events of Jesus' life. They select, arrange and modify material at their disposal to stress important themes—like the connection between Jesus and the Old Testament, the inclusion of gentiles in the kingdom and the nature of discipleship.

Mark's gospel was probably written for gentile Christians living in Rome. Could this audience have understood the various allusions to the Hebrew Bible worked into Mark's narrative? On the other hand, Mark's contemporaries might well have grasped a pattern of meaning that has gone unrecognized by modern Bible commentators: In Mark's gospel, the crucifixion procession is a kind of Roman triumphal march, with Jerusalem's Via Dolorosa replacing the Sacra Via of Rome. In this way, Mark presents Jesus' defeat and death, the moment of his greatest suffering and humiliation, as both literally and figuratively a *triumph*.

Here we will examine more closely the crucifixion procession as described in Mark 15:16-39 (see box, p. 62). But first let's look at the triumphal march, especially the features with which Mark's first-century A.D. Roman contemporaries would have been familiar.

The triumph was a celebration in which victorious generals and emperors paraded through Rome, putting their accomplishments on display for the populace. It evolved from Etruscan and Greek ceremonies calling for an appearance or epiphany, of Dionysus, the dying and rising god.[1] In the Athenian New Year festival, Dionysus, portrayed in costume by the king, was carried into the city in a formal procession, that culminated in a cry for the epiphany of the god (in Greek, *thriambos*; in Latin, *triumpe*). A bull was then sacrificed, and the king appeared as the god. In Greece, Zeus eventually supplanted Dionysus; the shift probably occurred because of Zeus's position as *king* of the gods.

The Roman historian Dio Cassius describes an early Roman triumph after which subsequent processions were patterned. First, the soldiers proclaimed a victorious general *imperator*, and the senate decreed a triumph. The triumphator appeared "arrayed in the triumphal dress and wearing armlets, with a laurel crown upon his head, and holding a branch in his right hand." He called together the people, praised the gathered soldiers, distributed gifts and then mounted a tower-shaped chariot, where a slave held a crown over his head. The triumphator was preceded into the city by captives displaying graphic representations of his victories. Finally, "the victorious general arrived at the Roman Forum, and after commanding that some of the captives be led to prison and put to death, he rode up to the Capitol. There he performed certain rites and made offerings and dined in the porticos up there, after which he departed homeward toward evening."[2]

The connection between the triumphator and Jupiter (the Roman equivalent of Zeus) is remarkable. The triumphal robe, a garment of regal purple embroidered with gold, and the gold laurel wreath were both borrowed from the statue of the god in the temple Jupiter Capitolinus. The face of the triumphator was painted red in imitation of the same statue. The crowd cried *triumpe*, a call for the manifestation of the god. During the Roman Republic, however, the triumphator was only recognized as under the tutelage of the god. The identification of the king with the deity would come later.

In the latter period of the Roman Republic, as successive triumphators attempted to align themselves with, and even upstage, military heroes of the past, the processions became more complex, overlaying traditional ceremonial elements with increasingly gaudy and lavish displays.[3] After about 20 B.C., the triumph became the exclusive privilege of the emperor. Now it was a tribute to an all-powerful individual, who, upon his accession, might well celebrate his conquest *of* Rome rather than his conquest *for* Rome or might manufacture any pretense for a display of power. Ultimately, for the mid-first-century tyrants Gaius (more familiarly known as Caligula) and Nero, this privilege brought the triumph together with the notion of the imperator's own deification. Thus the ceremony became reconnected with its roots as a display of the ruler as a god.

It is in this relation between triumph and deity that the most profound connection with the Gospel of Mark emerges. Even prior to Mark's gospel (before about 70 A.D.), Jesus was understood as a triumphator. In 2 Corinthians 2:14-15, Paul proclaims:

> Christ always leads us in triumphal procession, and through us spreads in every place the fragrance that comes from knowing him. For we are the aroma of Christ to God among those who are being saved and among those who are perishing.

Even the references to scent may evoke the image of first-century triumphs, which included the distribution of aromatic substances along the route of the procession to signify the preservation of the life of the triumphator and possibly the death of his captives, some of whom would be killed.[4] Whether or not Paul extends the metaphor, there can be no mistaking his allusion to Christ as triumphator.

Mark's crucifixion narrative contains a number of striking parallels to the Roman triumph. While the cumulative force of the comparison

[16]Then the soldiers led [Jesus] into the courtyard of the palace (that is, the governor's headquarters); and they called together the whole cohort. [17]And they clothed him in a purple cloak; and after twisting some thorns into a crown, they put it on him. [18]And they began saluting him, "Hail, King of the Jews!" [19]They struck his head with a reed, spat upon him, and knelt down in homage to him. [20]After mocking him, they stripped him of the purple cloak and put his own clothes on him. Then they led him out to crucify him.

[21]They compelled a passerby, who was coming in from the country, to carry his cross; it was Simon of Cyrene, the father of Alexander and Rufus. [22]Then they brought Jesus to the place called Golgotha (which means the place of a skull). [23]And they offered him wine mixed with myrrh; but he did not take it. [24]And they crucified him, and divided his clothes among them, casting lots to decide what each should take. [25]It was nine o'clock in the morning when they crucified him. [26]The inscription of the charge against him read, "The King of the Jews." [27]And with him they crucified two bandits, one on his right and one on his left. [29]Those who passed by derided him, shaking their heads and saying, "Aha! You who would destroy the Temple and build it in three days, [30]save yourself and come down from the cross!" [31]In the same way the chief priests, along with the scribes, were also mocking him among themselves and saying, "He saved others; he cannot save himself. [32]Let the Messiah, the King of Israel, come down from the cross now, so that we may see and believe." Those who were crucified with him also taunted him.

[33]When it was noon, darkness came over the whole land until three in the afternoon. [34]At three o'clock Jesus cried out with a loud voice, "*Eloi, Eloi, lema sabachthani?*" which means, "My God, my God, why have you forsaken me?" [35]When some of the bystanders heard it, they said, "Listen, he is calling for Elijah." [36]And someone ran, filled a sponge with sour wine, put it on a stick, and gave it to him to drink, saying, "Wait, let us see whether Elijah will come to take him down." [37]Then Jesus gave a loud cry and breathed his last. [38]And the curtain of the temple was torn in two, from top to bottom. [39]Now, when the centurion, who stood facing him, saw that in this way he breathed his last, he said, "Truly this man was God's Son!"

New Revised Standard Version

is significant, the most obvious allusions are made at the beginning of the narrative, perhaps signaling to Mark's audience that there is more to come for those "on the inside" (compare Mark 4:11).

Mark's narrative begins with the Roman soldiers leading Jesus into "the courtyard of the palace." The word Mark uses to refer to this place is *praetorium,* which could apply to military headquarters in general (for example, in Acts 23:35) but was also the common designation in Rome for the place and personnel of the imperial guard. The praetorian guard, which made or broke the power of emperors, was invariably present on the occasion of a triumph, and significantly, it was called together en masse. If it were not for this custom of mustering the praetorian guard, we might think that Mark's naming of the palace courtyard as the *praetorium* was simply an incidental detail. But Mark then tells us that "they called together the *whole* cohort." It would be extremely odd for the entire soldiery (at least 200 men) to be called together to mock and beat a single prisoner. Rather, we should consider the details here as carefully chosen to evoke a familiar occasion, namely, the gathering of the soldiery in preparation for a triumphal march.

Contemporaneous accounts of Roman triumphs suggest that Mark's description of Jesus' clothing ("They clothed him in a purple cloak; and after twisting some thorns into a crown, they put it on him" [Mark 15:17]) follows a formula. In one source after another, the triumphator is introduced clad in a ceremonial purple robe and a crown.[5] The wearing of purple was outlawed for anyone below equestrian rank. The only available robe of this kind for Jesus would belong to Pilate, but it is inconceivable that he would lend his garment to be spat on by soldiers. Along similarly practical lines, one must wonder where in the courtyard of a palace thorns would be available to make a crown. Are we to imagine that the soldiers delayed their mockery while someone went to look for a thornbush? The strangeness of these details, their likeness to the ceremonial garb of a triumphator and their combination with other details of the narrative suggest purpose rather than coincidence.[6]

Before the procession began, when the triumphator appeared in ceremonial garb, he would meet with the soldiers to receive their accolades. So in Mark's gospel the immediate sequel to the appearance of Jesus in royal garb is the mock homage of the soldiers ("They began saluting him"). Their shout, "Hail, King of the Jews!" (Mark 15:18), may in fact correspond to a formulaic response in a triumph.[7]

As the soldiers lead Jesus along the Via Dolorosa, they compel an onlooker, Simon, to bear the cross. Simon is identified as from Cyrene (a Greek colony in North Africa) and as the father of Alexander and Rufus, who were probably known to Mark's audience as church figures (Romans 16:13; 1 Timothy 1:20; 2 Timothy 4:14). The account of Simon's requisition by the soldiers as cross-carrier may serve simply to suggest the wearying effect of a prolonged procession. But it may also suggest another formulaic element in a triumph. A consistent feature in the numerous monuments depicting triumphs is the sacrificial bull, led along dressed and crowned to signify its identity with the triumphator. But the bull is not alone. In nearly every one of these depictions, walking alongside the bull is an official who carries over his shoulder a double-bladed ax, the instrument of the victim's death. The parallel might appear to be coincidental, but two remarkable details— Simon's link to the community of faith via his sons and his having just arrived from out of town—suggest that Mark envisions his role as divinely planned. Like the official who bears the ax, Simon carries the instrument of the sacrifice's—in this case Jesus'—death: the cross.

Crucifixions were common enough in the Roman world that major cities set aside special places for them. The crucified bodies, in various stages of suffering or decomposition, provided a public warning to potential malefactors. In Rome, the place was the Campus Esquilinus; in Jerusalem, it may have been either the site of the present Church of the Holy Sepulchre or on the Mount of Olives, across the Kidron Valley from the Temple. Mark gives the name of the place, *Golgotha*; then, untypically, he translates it for his readers: "which means the place of a skull." In Hebrew *Golgotha* denotes not an empty skull but more generally the head. Therefore, "place of the head" or perhaps "place of the death's-head" would be a more accurate rendering.[8]

Mark may be offering this translation simply to heighten the sense of the macabre. But there is a remarkable coincidence in the name of the place that may constitute another allusion to the triumph. Dionysius of Halicarnassus records the legend that, during the laying of a foundation for a temple on a certain Roman hill, a human head was discovered with its features intact. Soothsayers proclaimed:

> "Roman, tell your fellow citizens it is ordered by fate that the place
> in which you found the head shall be the head of all Italy," (and)
> since that time the place is called the Capitoline hill from the head
> that was found there; for the Romans call heads *capita*.[9]

The temple of Jupiter Capitolinus, or more simply the Capitolium, was the terminus of every Roman triumph. The procession would wind through the streets to the Forum, culminating in the ascent of the triumphator to the place of sacrifice—the place named after a death's-head. The name *Golgotha* may simply be a linguistic and historical coincidence, but to an audience prepared by the context of Mark's gospel to look for double meanings, it would be a glaring and meaningful coincidence: Golgotha was the Capitolium to which the triumphator ascended.

Before reaching Golgotha, the soldiers offer Jesus myrrhed wine, but he refuses to drink (Mark 15:23).[10] Why the offer of this expensive delicacy, why the refusal, and why interject this seemingly trivial detail here?

The supreme moment of the triumph is the moment of sacrifice, depicted in detail by numerous sculptors of the period. Just prior to the sacrifice of the bull, or in a few cases at the same time as the sacrifice, the triumphator was offered a cup of wine, which he would refuse and then pour on the altar (or, more rarely, on the bull itself). The wine obviously signifies the precious blood of the victim, and the links between triumphator, wine and victim signify their connection—which is also confirmed by the similar dress worn by both the triumphator and the bull. In other words, the bull is the god who dies and appears as the victor in the person of the triumphator.

All of this is shorthand for a long process of ritual development, but for our purposes the formulaic element is clear. At the crucial moment of a triumph, the moment of sacrifice, expensive wine is poured out. Significantly, the very next words in Mark's account are "and they crucified him." This again suggests a close association between wine and sacrifice. In an earlier scene in Mark's narrative, the Last Supper, Jesus himself makes the connection between the drinking of wine, sacrifice and triumphant renewal: "He said to them, 'This is my blood of the covenant, which is poured out for many. Truly I tell you, I will never again drink of the fruit of the vine until that day when I drink it new in the kingdom of God'" (Mark 14:24-25). The refusal of wine is one of the many details suggesting that the painful humiliation of the crucifixion is in fact a victorious triumph.

Another remarkable detail reported by Mark is that Jesus is executed with "two bandits, one on his right and one on his left" (Mark 15:27). This not only appears to be an unnecessary interruption of the narrative but also draws the attention of readers to the shamefulness of the crucifixion. Why accentuate the scandal of the cross by associating Jesus with criminals?

In the world of Mark's audience, placement on the right and left of an elevated person signified royal enthronement. Earlier in Mark's narration, for example, he tells us that two disciples request to be seated on Jesus' right and left when he is enthroned (Mark 10:37). In the triumph itself, the triumphator is normally alone but the exceptions are notable both because they occur at the point of elevation to the rostrum and because they occur very near to the time of Mark's writing.

Suetonius, a Roman historian of the early second century, records a triumph of the youthful Tiberius, who "took his seat beside Augustus between the two consuls."[11] In 44 A.D., Claudius returned to Rome after a military campaign and celebrated a triumph. "In this he followed precedent, even ascending the steps of the Capitol on his knees, with his sons-in-law supporting him on either side."[12] When Vitellius accepted the title *imperator* at Lugdunum in 68 A.D., he "spoke in praise of [his conquering generals] Valens and Caecina in public assembly and placed them on either side of his own curule chair."[13] In 71 A.D. Vespasian celebrated his triumph over the Jews with Titus beside him in the triumphal chariot and Domitian riding alongside;[14] the three then performed together the culminating events of the triumph.[15]

In each of these instances, a threesome appears elevated above an admiring throng in order to express power through solidarity. It is probable, then, that the crucifixion of criminals on either side of Jesus is a conscious expression of the mockery of his kingship on the part of the soldiers. That is, they are the mock equivalent of those displayed on either side of an enthroned ruler.

To summarize Mark's narrative as now decoded: The praetorian guard gathers early in the morning to proclaim the triumphator. They dress him in the purple triumphal garb and place a crown of laurel on his head. The soldiers shout in acclamation of his lordship ("Hail, King of the Jews [Mark 15:18]) and perform acts of homage to him. They accompany him through the streets of the city. The sacrifice walks alongside a person who carries the instrument of death. The procession ascends to the place of the (death's) head, where the sacrifice is to take place. The triumphator is offered ceremonial wine. He does not drink it but pours it out on the altar at the moment of sacrifice. Then, at the moment when he is lifted up before the people, at the moment of the sacrifice, the triumphator is again acclaimed as lord ("The King of the Jews" [Mark 15:26]), and his viceregents appear with him in confirmation of his glory. The epiphany of the triumphator is accompanied by a divine portent ("The curtain of the Temple was torn in two" [Mark 15:38]), confirming that he is one with the gods.

The opening sentence of Mark's gospel identifies Jesus as "the Son of God," but no human voice gives him that title until after he dies. Struck with wonder as he watches Jesus breathe his last, a Roman centurion gasps, "Truly this man was God's Son!" (Mark 15:39). The moment of Jesus' death, the moment of his sacrifice, is the culmination of Mark's parable of triumph. But Mark presents the crucifixion as an "anti-triumph"—with Jesus mocked and killed—to show that the seeming scandal of the cross is actually an exaltation of Christ.

Mark's anti-triumph, I would argue, was composed in reaction to the self-deification of the emperors Gaius (37-41 A.D.) and especially Nero (54-68 A.D.). Gaius would regularly visit the temple of Jupiter Capitolinus to engage in confidential chats with the deity.[16] He required that courtiers hail him as Jupiter and built a temple to his own godhead containing a statue with whom he regularly exchanged clothing. Similarly, Nero's conduct in public triumph confirms his own flirtation with divinity. At the culmination of one procession, King Tiridates paid obeisance to Nero by saying, "I have come to thee, my god, to worship thee as I do Mithras."[17] On this occasion, Nero was dressed in triumphal garb, and the canopy over his head depicted him in the attitude of the god, "driving a chariot, with golden stars gleaming all about him."[18] During another triumph, Nero was hailed as, among other things, Apollo and Divine Voice.[19]

As these events were occupying center stage in Rome, members of the Roman church were struggling to understand and communicate the notion that God had revealed himself in the person of Jesus, who was understood as both the Crucified One and the Coming One. It would have been natural for them to make comparisons between the Lord Christ and the Lord Caesar, and it would have been natural for them to look for evidence of God's sovereignty in Jesus' humility. Is it not plausible that Mark would arrange some of these details to hint at a correspondence between the mockery of Jesus and the empty, futile adoration of the *imperator*? For Mark, it is the mocked Jesus, not the gaudy Roman emperor, who is the true epiphanic triumphator.

1. H.S. Versnel, *Triumphus* (Leiden: Brill, 1970), pp. 235-300.

2. Dio Cassius 6.23 (see Zonaras 7.21). For other accounts, see Livy, *Epitome* 10.7.10; Juevenal, *Satires* 10.36; and Servius's commentary on Virgil's *Eclogues* 6.22.

3. See, for example, Livy, *Epitome* 1.10.5, 10.7.9; Dionysius of Halicarnassus, *Roman Antiquities* 2.34.2; Dio Cassius 51.21.8-9; and Suetonius, *Nero* 25.

4. See Suetonius, *Nero* 25.2; and Dio Cassius 6.23.

5. See, for example, Dio Cassius 62.4.3-62.6.2.

6. At the same time that Mark appeals to his gentile audience by utilizing imagery from the Roman triumphal march, he inserts allusions to the Hebrew Bible. After the Roman soldiers mockingly salute Jesus, his regal clothes are removed, and his own clothes are put back on him (Mark 15:20). Although this is inconsistent with the custom of the triumphator's wearing of the ceremonial robe throughout the procession, it is necessary to keep in motion another pattern of allusions—to Psalm 22, which speaks of one "scorned ... and despised by the people. All who see me mock at me" (verses 6-7). After crucifying Jesus, the Roman soldiers then cast lots for his garments. This is another allusion to Psalm 22: "They divide my clothes among themselves, and for my clothing they cast lots" (verse 18). The imagery drawn from this psalm reaches its dramatic climax just a few verses later in Mark's crucifixion narrative, after Jesus has been nailed to the cross: "Jesus cried out with a loud voice, '*Eloi, Eloi, lema sabachthani?*' which means, 'My God, my God, why have you forsaken me?'" (Mark 15:34). These are the first words of Psalm 22.

7. Although we do not have an explicit record of such a response, Suetonius may provide a hint when he reports that during a procession of Nero's, his escort "shouted that they were attendants of Augustus and the soldiers of his triumph" (*Nero* 6.25).

8. The Vulgate *calvaria* (as opposed to *caput*), the ambiguity of the English word "head," and the popular image associated with Gordon's Calvary may exert undue influence on modern translations.

9. Dionysius of Halicarnassus, *Roman Antiquities* 4.59-61; cf. Livy, *Epitome* 50.55.5-6.

10. Pliny describes myrrhed wine as the finest (*Naturalis Historia* 14.92). Sour wine or vinegar, as in Mark 15:36, was understood to deaden pain (Pliny, *Naturalis Historia* 23.24-27), but while the ancients often describe the sedative effect of myrrh alone or in combination with other ingredients, none ascribe such an effect for myrrhed wine. Wine mixed with myrrh was an expensive delicacy that probably was not understood to deaden pain.

11. Suetonius, *Tibullus* 17.

12. Dio Cassius 60.23.1.

13. Tacitus, *Histories* 2.59.

14. Josephus, *The Jewish War* 152.

15. Josephus, *The Jewish War* 153-157.

16. Suetonius, *Caligula* 22.3-4.

17. Dio Cassius 63.5.2.

18. Dio Cassius 63.6.2.

19. Dio Cassius 62.20.5.

CHAPTER FIVE

TRACING THE VIA DOLOROSA

Jerome Murphy-O'Connor

The Latin words *Via Dolorosa* mean the "Sorrowful Way." They were first used by the Franciscan Boniface of Ragusa in the second half of the 16th century as the name of the devotional walk through the streets of Jerusalem that retraced the route followed by Jesus as he carried his cross to Golgotha. It is also known as the *Via Crucis*, the "Way of the Cross." Today it is divided into 14 segments by a series of stops, called stations, where pilgrims pray (see maps, pp. 74-75). The fourteen stations are

(1) Jesus is condemned to death by Pontius Pilate (Mark 15:6-20).

(2) The cross is laid upon Jesus (John 19:17).

(3) Jesus falls for the first time.

(4) Jesus meets his mother, who collapses in shock (the spasm).

(5) Simon of Cyrene is forced to carry the cross (Mark 15:21).

(6) Veronica wipes the face of Jesus.

(7) Jesus falls for the second time.

(8) Jesus meets the women of Jerusalem (Luke 23:27-31).

(9) Jesus falls for the third time.

(10) Jesus is stripped of his garments (Mark 15:24).

(11) Jesus is nailed to the cross (Mark 15:24).

(12) Jesus dies (Mark 15:37).

(13) The body of Jesus is taken down from the cross (Mark 15:46).

(14) The body is laid in the tomb (Mark 15:46).

As you will readily see, no gospel references are appended to five stations (nos. 3, 4, 6, 7, 9). This immediately draws attention to a problem. The encounter of Jesus with his mother (no. 4) and with Veronica (no. 6), and the three falls (nos. 3, 7, 9), have no basis in Scripture. What guarantee do we have that they are authentic?

Once a note of skepticism has been introduced, other questions become inevitable. Can the other incidents be located so precisely? Is the street plan of Jerusalem the same as it was at the time of Jesus? Is the traditional starting point the authentic one? That is, the *praetorium* (headquarters) of Pilate, where Jesus was condemned, at the Antonia Fortress, as the present route assumes, or elsewhere?

Let us begin with the last question. When the Romans took direct control of Judea in 6 A.D., they made Caesarea Maritima their capital. The emperor's representative, in Judea a procurator, lived in a magnificent palace built there by Herod the Great, which thus became the Caesarea *praetorium*. The procurator came to Jerusalem on the occasion of the great Jewish feasts, when the population of the city more than doubled with the influx of pilgrims. The possibility of disturbances was evident. The procurator's troops could be used immediately to quell any threat to Roman authority.

In the Holy City the procurator had a choice of two residences— a palace built by Herod the Great, on the western side of the city, and the Antonia Fortress, on the eastern side just north of the Temple. Which did he choose? The palace is much more probable.

Normal Roman practice dictated that the procurator, Pontius Pilate, should opt for the palace on the west side of the city, on the site of the present Citadel inside Jaffa Gate, where remains of the palace have in fact been found. Occupying the palace of the previous ruler symbolized the transfer of power. Moreover the palace was much larger and more imposing than the Antonia, which was no more than a military barracks. It is absurd to imagine that Pilate would choose to occupy a second-rate residence and while his second-in-command lived in luxury at the palace.

Understandably, therefore, Philo of Alexandria (c. 20 B.C.– c. 50 A.D.) calls the palace of Herod the Great "the house of the procurators" and places Pilate there on the occasion of the event of the shields.[1] Josephus locates one of Pilate's successors, Gessius Florus, at the palace and describes an episode that has strong parallels with the condemnation of Jesus: "Florus took up his quarters at the palace, and on the next day had his tribunal set before it ... the soldiers caught many of the quiet people and brought them before Florus, whom he first scourged and then crucified."[2]

Thus, the *praetorium* mentioned in the Gospels as the residence of Pilate (Matthew 27:27; Mark 15:16; John 18:28,33, 19:9) should be identified with the palace on the western side of the city. This is confirmed by John 19:13, which tells us that the place where Pilate judged Jesus was called *lithostroton* in Greek and *gabbatha* in Hebrew. The two words do not mean the same thing. *Lithostroton* means "a paved area." The meaning of *gabbatha* is not certain, but the underlying Aramaic (not Hebrew) root *gbh* or *gb'* means "to be high, to protrude."[3] Hence, the idea of elevation. When used absolutely, as here, the best translation is probably the "high point."[4] That turns our attention to the palace, the highest point on Jerusalem's western hill,[5] which Josephus consistently calls "the upper city" because it was much higher than the eastern hill.[6]

Thus the historical Way of the Cross started in the area of the modern Citadel, just inside Jaffa Gate. From the palace Jesus would have been led across the upper forum[7] into a street leading to the Gennath Gate,[8] in the first (north) wall of Herodian Jerusalem. The centurion in charge of the execution party had selected an abandoned

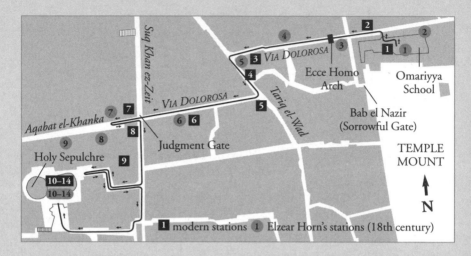

The Via Dolorosa, or Sorrowful Way (indicated on the map at right), is the 16th-century name given to the path Christians have traditionally claimed Jesus followed on the way to the crucifixion. Today, 14 stations along the way commemorate the last events of Jesus' life—from the judgment of Pilate (1) to the burial of Jesus (14). The present-day Via Dolorosa developed out of a devotional walk first introduced by the Franciscans in Jerusalem in the 14th century. By the 16th century, several European cities had their own re-creations of the Way of the Cross, and the route became increasingly disconnected from the topography of Jerusalem. In the 18th century, the Franciscan Elzear Horn, who ministered in the Holy Land from 1724 to 1744, redrew the Via Dolorosa based on Jerusalem's actual street plan (see his drawing, p. 82). The modern Via Dolorosa remains close to Horn's vision (the modern stations and Horn's are marked on the map, above).

Both plans have little to do with the actual route Jesus would have taken, however, in that they locate Pilate's praetorium in the east side of the city (specifically, at the Antonia Fortress, a barracks attached to the north end of the Temple Mount). Author Murphy-O'Connor suggests the praetorium was instead on the western side of town, in a lavish palace built by Herod. From there, Jesus would have been led out the Gennath Gate to Golgotha (now inside the Old City walls and the site of the Holy Sepulchre Church).

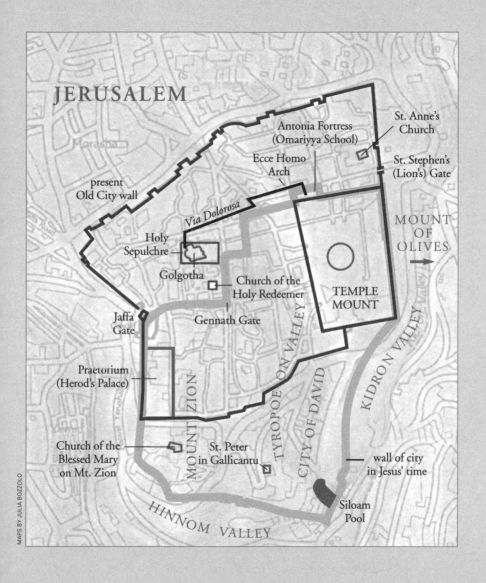

JERUSALEM

present
Old City wall

Antonia Fortress
(Omariyya School)

Ecce Homo
Arch

St. Anne's
Church

St. Stephen's
(Lion's) Gate

Via Dolorosa

Holy
Sepulchre

Golgotha

Church of the
Holy Redeemer

Gennath Gate

Jaffa
Gate

MOUNT
OF
OLIVES

TEMPLE
MOUNT

Praetorium
(Herod's Palace)

MOUNT ZION

TYROPOEON VALLEY

CITY OF DAVID

KIDRON VALLEY

Church of the
Blessed Mary
on Mt. Zion

St. Peter
in Gallicantu

wall of city
in Jesus' time

Siloam
Pool

HINNOM VALLEY

MAPS BY JULIA BOZZOLO

quarry just outside the gate as the place of execution. On the east side of the quarry, a rock projection called Golgotha somehow gave the impression of a skull (Mark 15:22). There the Roman soldiers raised the cross. In April the bed of the quarry was a sheen of green. After the winter rains, windblown seeds flourished in soil deposited by a century of sandstorms. In the west wall of the quarry, an entrepreneur had cut a catacomb, in which tombs opened off a central passage. The disciples who took the body of Jesus from the cross used one of these tombs as a temporary measure. It was close, and the Sabbath was about to begin (John 19:40-42). That particular Friday was the Day of Preparation for Passover (John 19:31).

The quarry in which Jesus was crucified and buried is today covered by the Church of the Holy Sepulchre.[9] Thus the last five stations of the Via Dolorosa (the 10th to the 14th), which are located within the church, have a valid claim to authenticity, even though the floor is much higher than the floor of the quarry.

It is equally clear, however, that of the first nine stations, the four mentioned in the Gospels cannot possibly be correct. They have to be located on the other side of the city, between the Holy Sepulchre and Jaffa Gate.

What happened? How did the Via Dolorosa come into being?

The present Via Dolorosa developed out of a circuit of the Jerusalem holy places that the Franciscans developed for pilgrims in the 14th century. A Roman Catholic religious order founded by St. Francis of Assisi in 1209, the Franciscans were made custodians of the Holy Land in 1335. This privilege carried two major duties. First, they had to ensure the performance of the Latin liturgical services in the Holy Sepulchre in Jerusalem and in the Church of the Nativity in Bethlehem. Second, they were responsible for pilgrims from Europe, in a double sense. They were the intermediaries with the local authorities in case of any dispute, and they served as guides to the holy places. In the 14th century, pilgrims usually spent between ten and fourteen days in Jerusalem. In order to guarantee that they saw everything systematically, the Franciscans over the years developed a careful routine.

The tour was circular and based in sound common sense. It was given added authority, however, by the legend that Mary had followed the same route each day during her last years in Jerusalem in order to visit the places associated with her son. Such reverence on her part made it difficult for pilgrims to disagree with the route laid down by their guide! The pilgrims' path started at the Franciscan Monastery on Mt. Sion. They visited the house of Caiaphas and the palace of Annas, both then located on the western side of the city, en route to the Holy Sepulchre. Then they crossed to the east side of the city, which they left to climb the Mount of Olives. From there they descended to the Pool of Siloam, then ended the circuit by ascending the steep slope that brought them back to Mt. Sion.

This brief description gives no hint of the amount of detail crammed into every step of the way. The credulity, simplicity and vivid imagination of pilgrims during the late Middle Ages assigned a tangible location to every biblical incident and legendary development. On being shown the house of the rich man (Luke 16:19-31), for example, Robert Curzon heard a guide give a considered, affirmative reply to a pilgrim who questioned whether the dogs on the street were the descendants of those who had licked the sores of Lazarus (Luke 16:21)![10]

Interesting as the complete circuit is, we must focus on the section that came to be recognized as the Via Dolorosa. After leaving the Holy Sepulchre, as they headed east across the city, the pilgrims were shown a series of mementos of Jesus, namely, the flagstone in the courtyard of the Holy Sepulchre where Jesus fell; the Judgment gate, to which the death notice had been affixed and by which Jesus left the city for Golgotha (this gate was important in order to underline the point that the site of the Holy Sepulchre had been outside the city at the time of Jesus); the tavern where the soldier got the sour wine (Mark 15:36); the house of Veronica; the house of the rich man (Luke 16:19-31); the intersection at which the cross was transferred from Jesus to Simon of Cyrene (Mark 15:21); the place where Jesus encountered the women of Jerusalem (Luke 23:27-31); the steps where Mary collapsed when she mounted to see her son; the arch where Jesus was condemned; the school Mary had attended as a girl; the house of Pilate (Mark 15:1); the house of Herod Antipas (Luke 23:6-12); the house of Simon the Pharisee, where Mary Magdalene was pardoned (Luke 7:36-50); the Beautiful Gate of the Temple (Acts 3:2); the Temple of the Lord (Luke 2:27); the house of Anne, where Mary was born; the pool at the Sheep Gate (John 5:2); and finally the gate leading to the Valley of Jehoshaphat (Kidron Valley).[11] At each place the pilgrims stopped to pray. There was no critical discussion of historical authenticity. The guide was a moralizing preacher who exploited the awe with which the pilgrims looked at what they were shown.

As the 15th century progressed, a feeling grew that the section between the Holy Sepulchre and the house of Pilate should have a special status in the pilgrim circuit because it was here that Jesus slowly died for our sins. This recognition brought with it the realization that the traditional direction (from the Holy Sepulchre to the house of Pilate) should be reversed. It would be more appropriate, and spiritually more beneficial, to begin at the house of Pilate and to end at the Holy Sepulchre. Then the pilgrim could walk in the footsteps of Jesus.

This new devotional exercise was well established by 1530, when it was described by a Spanish Franciscan Antonio of Aranda. At this stage, however, there were only three intermediate stations between the house of Pilate and the Holy Sepulchre: (1) Jesus encounters Mary, who collapses; (2) Simon of Cyrene takes the cross from Jesus, who addresses the women of Jerusalem; and (3) Veronica wipes the face of Jesus.[12] Strict Ottoman controls in the 16th century made any public manifestation of Christian piety in the streets impossible. The pilgrims walked in small groups and prayed silently at the different stations.

The experience of the Via Dolorosa left an indelible mark on visitors to Jerusalem. A number were so profoundly moved that when they returned to Europe they tried to replicate the conditions of the Way of the Cross, so that those who had not made the pilgrimage could reap the same spiritual benefits. Thus the next phase in the development of the Via Dolorosa took place in Europe, where creativity was not blocked by tradition. The Muslim authorities in Jerusalem tolerated what was well established, but innovations were frowned upon. Only in Europe could the imagination of believers be given free rein. Inevitably, the number of stations increased.

The first effort in this sense was that of a Spanish Dominican, Blessed Alvarez of Cordova (died 1420), who visited Jerusalem sometime before 1405. When he built the Monastery of Scala Coeli in Cordova, he incorporated eight chapels painted with the scenes of the Passion that he had seen in Jerusalem. A German, Martin Ketzel, had a much more dramatic solution. Having lost his notes on the distances between the stations in Jerusalem, he undertook a second pilgrimage to the Holy City in 1472 to remedy this defect. When he got back to Nuremberg, he set up an open-air Via Dolorosa, beginning with a house of Pilate at one of the gates of the city and terminating in the cemetery of St. John. The seven intermediate stations were marked with sculptures by Adam Krafft. Each one had a descriptive title and noted the number of steps from the previous station. These stations were (1) Jesus encounters Mary; (2) Simon of Cyrene carries the cross; (3) Jesus addresses the women of Jerusalem; (4) Veronica wipes the face of Jesus; (5) Jesus is struck by bystanders; (6) Jesus falls; and (7) Mary holds the dead body of Jesus. In each the sculptor depicted Jesus on the point of falling beneath the weight of the cross. In consequence, the stations became known as the "Seven Falls."

This representation of the Way of the Cross had a tremendous impact and was imitated at Romans, in France; Fribourg, in Switzerland; Bamberg, in Germany; and throughout Belgium. The one representation at Louvain became the most important because, indirectly, it gave rise to two books that were to be decisive in giving the Via Dolorosa in Jerusalem its present form. It first inspired Jan

Pascha to write his *Spiritual Journey*, which was published by Peter Calentyn in 1563.[13] This detailed spiritual reflection on the route of the Passion was based on the reports of pilgrims and supplemented by the Gospels. It is the first to use the expression the "Way of the Cross." In turn, Pascha's work stimulated a Dutch scholar, Christian van Adrichom, to attempt a scientific effort, *Description of Jerusalem at the Time of Christ*, which first appeared in 1584. This book was quickly translated into all the European languages and remained the classical manual of the topography of Jerusalem up until the 19th century.[14]

Both Pascha and van Adrichom give the following stations: (1) the house of Pilate; (2) Jesus receives the cross; (3) Jesus falls for the first time; (4) Jesus encounters Mary, who collapses; (5) Simon of Cyrene carries the cross; (6) Veronica wipes the face of Jesus; (7) Jesus falls for the second time; (8) Jesus addresses the women of Jerusalem; (9) Jesus

The Franciscan Bernardino Amico relied on his firsthand knowledge of the Holy Land to create accurate, measured plans of Jerusalem buildings in 1591. He produced three drawings of the Via Dolorosa, including this middle scene, which shows the judgment of Pilate under the Ecce Homo arch (at left) and the chapel (at right) where Jesus encountered Mary and she collapsed.

FROM *PLANS OF THE SACRED EDIFICES OF THE HOLY LAND*

falls for the third time; (10) Jesus is stripped of his garments; (11) Jesus is nailed to the cross; (12) Jesus dies on the cross; (13) Jesus' body is taken down from the cross; and (14) Jesus is laid to rest in the tomb.[15]

This was to become the classic list, but initially it had little impact on practice in Jerusalem. It was implicitly criticized by the Franciscan Bernardino Amico, who produced the first measured plans of buildings in Jerusalem in 1591. He divides the Via Dolorosa into three segments. His first drawing shows the palace of Pilate, where Jesus was scourged. The second drawing depicts the arch of Pilate, where Jesus was judged, and the Chapel of the Collapse of the Mother of Jesus, where Jesus met Mary. The final drawing is more complex. It shows a street on which are located Simon's assumption of the cross, the encounter with the women of Jerusalem, the house of Veronica and the Judgment Gate.[16]

The same tactful but definite refutation appears in the *Explanation of the Holy Land*, published in 1639 by another Franciscan, Francesco Quaresmio.[17] He introduces the subject thus, "The sixth walk [in Jerusalem] is the way of the cross or the sorrowful way in which the eight principal sites venerated by pilgrims are recalled and described."[18] These are (1) the palace of Pilate; (2) the flagellation of Christ; (3) the palace of Herod; (4) the Ecce Homo arch; (5) the Chapel of the Collapse; (6) the corner where Simon took the cross from Jesus, who then speaks to the women of Jerusalem; (7) the house of Veronica; and (8) the Judgment Gate. This was the last station. Quaresmio comments, "This is the end." The route that Jesus had followed from the Judgment Gate to Golgotha could no longer be retraced. What then had been open country was now completely built up. To get to the Holy Sepulchre, pilgrims had to go through streets that had no traditional connection with Jesus.

In the 17th century, those who made the devotional exercise of the 14-station Way of the Cross popularized by Pascha and van Adrichom in Europe were convinced that it accurately reflected the route in Jerusalem. Not surprisingly, therefore, the pilgrims who came to the Holy City were shocked to find that the Jerusalem tradition

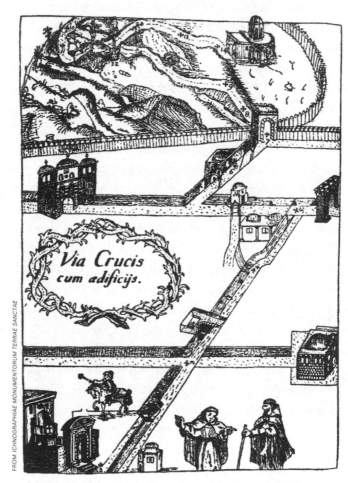

FROM *ICHNOGRAPHIAE MONUMENTORUM TERRAE SANCTAE*

The Via Dolorosa is seen from the east in Franciscan Elzear Horn's 18th-century etching. The route begins at Pilate's palace (lower left), passes under the Ecce Homo arch, jogs left, and then continues on to the Holy Sepulchre (at top). All 14 stations along Horn's route are numbered on the map on page 74.

was different. They were particularly disappointed that the Via Dolorosa ended at the Judgment Gate. They expected it to terminate at the Holy Sepulchre. The explanations of the Franciscans fell on deaf ears, and frustrated anger implicitly condemned the competence of the guides. This situation could not be permitted to continue. Individual Franciscans began altering their tours to accommodate the expectations of the pilgrims regarding the number and order of the stations.

The final stage of this process is recorded by the Franciscan Elzear Horn, who ministered in the Holy Land from 1724 to 1744. He was heavily influenced by van Adrichom but corrected the latter's fantastic vision of the topography of Jerusalem (which van Adrichom had never visited!) by adapting it to the actual street plan of the city.[19] (See drawing, opposite, and the map on p. 74.)

Let us compare Horn's stations with the ones followed by today's pilgrims. The two lists are identical except where noted: (1) Pilate passes judgment: in the courtyard of the Omariyya School; (2) the cross is laid on Jesus: in the street outside the school—the station used to be about 250 feet east of the present site, outside the Monastery of the Flagellation; (3) Jesus falls for the first time: at the crossroads just east of the Ecce Homo arch—it is now at the northern junction of the Via Dolorosa and the Tariq el-Wad; (4) Jesus encounters his mother, who collapses: at the junction of the little street just east of the Armenian Catholic Church—it is now some 65 feet south of this church on the Tariq el-Wad; (5) Simon takes the cross: at the northern junction of the Via Dolorosa and the Tariq el-Wad—it is now at the southern junction; (6) Veronica wipes the faces of Jesus: in the middle of the section of the Via Dolorosa linking the Tariq el-Wad and the Suq Khan ez-Zeit; (7) Jesus falls for the second time: at the junction of the Via Dolorosa and the Suq Khan ez-Zeit; (8) Jesus addresses the women of Jerusalem: under the vaulted area of Aqabat el-Khanqa (this was Horn's most significant departure from the Jerusalem tradition, for this event had always been associated with the assumption of the cross by Simon of Cyrene); (9) Jesus falls for the third time: further up Aqabat el-Khanqa—today it is at the entrance to the Coptic Orthodox Patriarchate; (10-14) all within the Holy Sepulchre.

We began this story of how the present form of the Via Dolorosa came into being with the pilgrim circuit established by the Franciscans in the 14th century because that is the direct ancestor. The places on that pilgrim circuit, however, did not spring out of nowhere. They belonged to a much older tradition, which we must now look at briefly.

Even though there had been a strong Christian presence in Jerusalem during the first three centuries,[20] the Christianization of the city took place only in the fourth century. At that time, what had been an essentially private mode of worship became an overtly public one. In Jerusalem, Christians claimed their sacred space by moving in procession as they commemorated events in the life of Jesus.[21] For example, in the late fourth century, on the night of Holy Thursday, which commemorates the Last Supper (Mark 14:12-26) and the prayer of Jesus in Gethsemane (Mark 14:32-42), Christians assembled at the Eleona church on the Mount of Olives.[22] Then after services at the Imbomon (now the Mosque of the Ascension of Jesus) and at Gethsemane, they went without pause across the city for a dawn service in the courtyard of the Holy Sepulchre.[23] Even though the ceremony commemorated part of the Passion of Jesus, there was no intention of retracing his exact steps. The only feasible route from Gethsemane to the Holy Sepulchre was the one running along the northern side of the Temple.

In the eighth century, the same Holy Thursday procession followed a different route. From Gethsemane it went along the south wall of the Temple to the house of Caiaphas (today the Church of St. Peter in Gallicantu), then to the *praetorium* at the Church of Holy Wisdom, somewhere in the upper Tyropoeon Valley (the exact location is unknown), and finally to the courtyard of the Holy Sepulchre.[24] At this time there appears to have been a more deliberate intention to follow the movements of Jesus in the last hours of his life, but the walk was considered merely one liturgical service among others. It was not given a special character.

Growing interest in the events of the Passion of Jesus was stimulated in the 11th century when the Fatimids forbade Christian processions in the streets. Resentment fostered devotion; people always want to do what is forbidden. Thus when the Holy Sepulchre was restored by the emperor Constantine Monomachus in 1048, it incorporated a series of chapels dedicated to the Passion of Christ. They included the prison of Christ, the column at which he was scourged, the crowning with thorns and the division of his garments. This unsatisfactory solution was abandoned in the 12th century when Crusader control made it possible for Christians to again have public processions. Memory, however, had weakened in the interval. Moreover, the Crusaders were not very tolerant of the customs of the eastern church. The result was a serious difference of opinion among western Christians when the processions resumed.

Theoderic, a German monk who visited the Holy Land between 1169 and 1174, reports the location of Pilate's condemnation of Jesus as being "in front of the Church of the Blessed Mary on Mt. Sion." He continues, "From this place the Lord was taken out through the city wall, and round to Calvary. Then there were gardens there, but now the place is built over."[25] In terms of what we have seen above regarding the historical circumstances of the trial and condemnation of Jesus at Herod's palace at Mr. Sion, this is certainly the most authentic version of the Via Dolorosa to have appeared in Jerusalem. Theoderic locates Mary's encounter with Jesus, and her subsequent collapse, in the area now occupied by the Lutheran Redeemer Church.[26]

Although Theoderic formally places the beginnings of the Via Dolorosa on Mt. Sion, he twice mentions "the house of Pilate, which is next to the house of Saint Anne the Mother of our Lady, and near the Pool of the Sheep."[27] His contemporaries believed that the wood of the cross was taken from this pool,[28] which is now in the grounds of St. Anne's church, just inside St. Stephen's (the Lion's) Gate, on the eastern side of the Holy City. These two elements made it possible for the Templars and the Augustinian Canons, who controlled the Temple Mount, to develop a Via Dolorosa that began on the east side of Jerusalem, as does the present one.

They located the palaces of Caiaphas and Annas roughly on the site of the Antonia, north of the Temple. The flagstones on the northern end of the Temple Mount became the *lithostroton* "pavement" on which Pilate set up his judgment seat. In this version of the Via Dolorosa, Jesus, carrying his cross, left the Temple area by the Sorrowful Gate (today Bab al-Nazir) and went directly west to Golgotha via the modern Ala ed-Din and Aqabat et-Takiya.[29]

A succession of Latin Patriarchs apparently stayed neutral in the struggle that pitted the western Via Dolorosa against the eastern. No public procession was ever scheduled for Good Friday during the Crusader period.[30]

After the Arabs resumed control of the Temple Mount, which again became the Haram esh-Sharif in 1187, they made it impossible for the eastern Via Dolorosa to cut across the northwest corner of the paved esplanade. The partisans of this eastern version of the Via Dolorosa simply moved the judgment place of Pilate up to the Antonia. The Sorrowful Gate became only a memory, and the street outside was no longer used. It became more convenient to use a parallel street further north, which eventually became the modern Via Dolorosa.

The entire lack of interest in the western Via Dolorosa in the post-Crusade period is one of the minor mysteries of Jerusalem. One can only guess at the explanation. Saladin permitted a number of Latin clergy to return to the Holy Sepulchre, but only during the truce of 1229 to 1244 was there a significant Latin presence in the Holy City. The size of the Christian community left no room for divisions. A choice between the western and eastern Via Dolorosa had to be made, and it was inevitable that the eastern Via Dolorosa should be the one to survive. The austerity of the western Via Dolorosa could not compete with the variety of gospel and legendary associations attached to the eastern Via Dolorosa. The one dramatic episode of the western route, the encounter of Jesus with Mary, could be, and in fact was, easily integrated into the eastern route, which in addition localized the encounter with Veronica. A brief review of the development of this legend will serve as a graphic illustration of the type of popular piety that has given the Via Dolorosa its present form.

The fourth-century church historian Eusebius of Caesarea records having seen a statue of Jesus with the woman whose hemorrhage he had cured (Mark 5:24-34). It stood outside her house in Caesarea Philippi (modern Banias).[31] Her gratitude is recorded by the fourth-century Acts of Pilate, in which she appears as a character witness at Jesus' trial before Pilate: "And a woman called Bernice (Latin, Veronica), crying out from a distance, said, 'I had an issue of blood and I touched the hem of his garment, and the issue of blood, which I had for twelve years, ceased.' The Jews said, 'We have a law not to permit a woman to give testimony.'"[32] This slender connection with Pilate, of course, is the basis for Veronica's appearance on the Via Dolorosa, but by that stage the story had been greatly embroidered.[33]

According to a seventh-century version, Veronica wanted to have a portrait of Jesus and asked him to sit for a painter. Instead Jesus miraculously imprinted his face on a piece of cloth, which ended up in Rome. Its presence in the Eternal City is accounted for as follows. The emperor Tiberius was ill. He had heard of a miracle worker in Palestine who cured by a word, so the emperor sent an emissary to bring him to Rome. The emperor was not aware that Pilate had just had Jesus killed. A terrified Pilate did not know what to say to the imperial messenger, but Veronica bailed him out by offering to bring the image of Jesus' face to Rome. It cured the emperor. Thereafter the cloth was held in great honor in the Eternal City, where in the 12th century it attracted new legends.

According to one version, Veronica became ill again, but this time her condition was much more serious. She had leprosy. Though desperate for another miracle, she did not dare approach the cross on which Jesus was hanging. Mary, however, waved her forward and used Veronica's veil to wipe the face of Jesus. His face was imprinted on it. Veronica replaced her veil, and its touch cured her. This 13th-century version appears in a new form a century later. Veronica, on her way to the market, took pity on Jesus as he struggled under his cross and used her veil to wipe the perspiration from his face. When she took it back, the face of Jesus was imprinted on it. This version of the legend became the dominant one because it was adopted by the mystery plays so popular in medieval Europe. Inevitably, pilgrims expected to find the event commemorated in Jerusalem, and it became part of the Via Dolorosa.

The Via Dolorosa is defined not by history but by faith. It is the achievement of generations of Christians who desired above all to be in contact with what was tangible in the life of Christ. This is why they came on pilgrimage. This is why they asked, Where did this or that happen? As they stood in those places, their imaginations brought him alive before them. They traveled in hope. They found him in prayer.

1. Philo, *Legation to Gaius* 299-306. To annoy the Jews, Pilate erected in Herod's palace in the Holy City gilt shields with his own name and that of the Roman emperor, Tiberius. When the Jews protested, the emperor ordered the shields to be moved to the temple of Augustus in Caesarea.

2. Josephus, *The Jewish War* 2.301-306.

3. Raymond E. Brown, *The Death of the Messiah: From Gethsemane to the Grave*, Anchor Bible Reference Library (New York: Doubleday, 1994), p. 845.

4. See in particular Pierre Benoit, "Prétoire, Lithostrothon et Gabbatha," *Revue Biblique* 59 (1962), pp. 548-550.

5. Josephus calls it the "upper palace" (*Jewish War* 2.429) to distinguish it from the old Hasmonean palace on the eastern slope of the Tyropoeon Valley.

6. Josephus, *Jewish War* 5.137, cf. 1.402; and *Antiquities of the Jews* 15.318.

7. Josephus, *Jewish War* 2.305,315, 5.137.

8. Josephus, *Jewish War* 5.146.

9. The definitive study is that of Virgilio C. Corbo, O.F.M., *Il Santo Sepolcro di Gerusalemme: Aspetti archeologici dalle origini ai periodo crociato* (Jerusalem: Franciscan Printing Press, 1981-1982).

10. Hilda F.F.M. Prescott, *Friar Felix at Large: A Fifteenth-Century Pilgrimage to the Holy Land* (New Haven: Yale University Press, 1960), p. 124.

11. Louis-Hugues Vincent and Felix-Marie Abel, *Jérusalem nouvelle* (Paris: Gabalda, 1922), p. 625.

12. Vincent and Abel, *Jérusalem nouvelle*, p. 626.

13. Reinhold Röhricht, *Bibliotheca Geographica Palaestinae: Chronologisches Verzeichniss der auf die Geographie des Heiligen Landes bezüglichen Literatur von 333 bis 1878 und Versuch einer Cartographie* (Berlin: Reuther, 1890), p. 180.

14. Röhricht, *Bibliotheca*, p. 209.

15. Vincent and Abel, *Jérusalem nouvelle*, p. 632.

16. Bernardino Amico, *Plans of the Sacred Edifices of the Holy Land*, trans. by T. Bellorini, O.F.M., and E. Hoade, O.F.M., with a preface and notes by B. Bagatti, O.F.M. (Jerusalem: Franciscan Press, 1953), pp. 78-86.

17. Röhricht, *Bibliotheca*, p. 239.

18. Francesco Quaresmio, *Elucidatio Terrae Sanctae*, 2.138, quoted in Vincent and Abel, *Jérusalem nouvelle*, p. 633 n. 1.

19. Elzear Horn, *Ichnographiae Monumentorum Terrae Sanctae (1724-1744)*, 2nd ed. of the Latin text with English version by Hoade, and preface and notes by Bagatti (Jerusalem: Franciscan Press, 1962), pp. 142-143.

20. See Jerome Murphy-O'Connor, "Pre-Constantinian Christian Jerusalem," in *The Christian Heritage in the Holy Land*, ed. A. O'Mahony, G. Gunner and K. Hintlian (London: Scorpion Cavendish, 1995), pp. 13-21.

21. See in particular John Baldovin, *The Urban Character of Christian Worship: The Origins, Development, and Meaning of Stational Liturgy* (Rome: Gregorian, 1987), pp. 45-104.

22. See the excavation report, Vincent, "L'église de l'Eleona," *Revue Biblique* 8 (1911), pp. 219-265; and his subsequent observation in "L'Eleona: Sanctuaire primitif de l'Ascension," *Revue Biblique* 64 (1957), pp. 48-71.

23. John Wilkinson, *Egeria's Travels to the Holy Land*, rev. ed. (Jerusalem: Ariel, 1981), pp. 75, 134-136.

24. Vincent and Abel, *Jérusalem nouvelle*, p. 610.

25. Wilkinson, with Joyce Hill and W.F. Ryan, *Jerusalem Pilgrimage, 1099-1185* (London: Hakluyt Society, 1988), pp. 300-301.

26. Wilkinson, *Jerusalem Pilgrimage*, p. 288.

27. Wilkinson, *Jerusalem Pilgrimage*, p. 278, cf. p. 301.

28. This was one of the most popular legends in the Middle Ages. A tree from Paradise found its way into the hands of Solomon, who honored it until he was told that from it would hang a man who would destroy the kingdom. He hid it at the bottom of a pool, which had dried out at the same time of Jesus' execution. See A. Wilmart, "La légende du bois de la croix," *Revue Biblique* 36 (1927), pp. 226-236; and Wilkinson, *Jerusalem Pilgrimage*, p. 75.

29. Vincent and Abel, *Jérusalem nouvelle*, pp. 612-613.

30. Vincent and Abel, *Jérusalem nouvelle*, p. 614.

31. Eusebius, *History of the Church* 7.18.

32. E. Hennecke and W. Schneemelcher, *New Testament Apocrypha*, trans. and ed. R. McL. Wilson (London: Lutterworth, 1959), vol.1, p. 457.

33. What follows is based on Vincent and Abel, *Jérusalem nouvelle*, pp. 618-620.

CHAPTER SIX

THE ARCHAEOLOGICAL EVIDENCE FOR CRUCIFIXION

Vassilios Tzaferis

From ancient literary sources we know that tens of thousands of people were crucified in the Roman Empire. In Palestine alone, the figure ran into the thousands. Yet until 1968 not a single victim of this horrifying method of execution had been uncovered archaeologically.

In that year I excavated the only victim of crucifixion ever discovered. He was a Jew, of a good family, who may have been convicted of a political crime. He lived in Jerusalem shortly after the turn of the era and sometime before the Roman destruction of Jerusalem in 70 A.D.

In the period following the Six Day War—when the Old City and East Jerusalem were newly under Israeli jurisdiction—a great deal of construction was undertaken. Accidental archaeological discoveries by construction crews were frequent. When that occurred, either my colleagues at the Israel Department of Antiquities and Museums or I would be called in; part of our job was to investigate these chance discoveries.

In late 1968, the then director of the department, Dr. Avraham Biran, asked me to check some tombs that had been found northeast of Jerusalem in an area called Giv'at ha-Mivtar. A crew from the Ministry of Housing had accidentally broken into some burial

ZEV RADOVAN

A large iron nail pierces the heel bone of a young Jewish man, in his mid- to late 20s, who was crucified outside Jerusalem in the first century A.D. The man's bones are the only remains of a crucifixion victim ever to be recovered from antiquity. That the bones were found in an ossuary (a box for bones) in a family burial cave suggests he was not a common thief; the excavator believes he was probably guilty of a political crime.

chambers and discovered the tombs. After we looked at the tombs, it was decided that I would excavate four of them.

The tombs were part of a huge Jewish cemetery of the Second Temple period (second century B.C. to 70 A.D.), extending from Mt. Scopus in the east to the Sanhedriya tombs in the northwest. Like most of the tombs of this period, the tomb I will focus on here was a cave-like cutting into the soft limestone that abounds in Jerusalem. The tomb consisted of two rooms or chambers, each with burial niches.

This particular tomb (which we call Tomb No. 1) was a typical Jewish tomb, just like many others found in Jerusalem. On the outside, in front of the entrance to the tomb, was a forecourt (which, unfortunately, had been badly damaged). The entrance itself was blocked by a stone slab and led to a large, carved-out chamber, nearly 10 feet square (Chamber A on the plan on p. 96). On three sides of the chamber were stone benches, intentionally left by the carver of the chamber. The fourth wall contained two openings leading down to another, lower chamber (Chamber B on the plan) that was similar in design to the first but had no benches. When we found Chamber B, its entrance was still blocked with a large stone slab.

Each of the two chambers contained burial niches that scholars call *loculi* (singular, *loculus*), about 5 to 6 feet long and 1 to 1.5 feet wide. In Chamber A, there were four loculi and in Chamber B, eight—two on each side. In Chamber B the two loculi carved into the wall adjacent to Chamber A were cut under the floor of Chamber A.

Some of the loculi were sealed by stone slabs; others were blocked by small undressed stones that had been covered with plaster. In Chamber B, in the floor by the entrance to Chamber A, a child's bones had been buried in a small pit. The pit was covered by a flat stone slab, similar to the ossuary lids I shall describe later.

Nine of the 12 loculi in the two tomb chambers contained skeletons, usually only one skeleton to a loculus. However, three of the loculi (Loculi 5, 7 and 9) contained ossuaries. Ossuaries are small boxes (about 16 to 28 inches long, 12 to 20 inches wide and 10 to 16 inches high) used for the secondary burial of bones. During this period, it was customary to collect the bones of the deceased after the body had been buried for almost a year and the flesh had decomposed. The bones were then reinterred in an ossuary. The practice of collecting bones in ossuaries had a religious significance that was probably connected with a belief in the resurrection of the dead. But this custom was also a practical measure; it allowed a tomb to be used for a prolonged period. As new burials became necessary, the bones of earlier burials were removed and placed in an ossuary. Reburial in an ossuary was, however, a privilege for the few; not every Jewish family could afford them. Most families reburied the bones of their dead in pits. The use of stone ossuaries probably began during the Herodian dynasty (which began in 37 B.C.) and ended in the second half of the second century A.D.

Thousands of ossuaries have been found in cemeteries around Jerusalem. Most, like the ones we found, are carved from soft local limestone. The workmanship varies. Some that we found in the tomb have a smooth finish over all their surfaces, including the lids. Others, especially the larger ossuaries, are cruder; the surfaces were left unsmoothed and the marks of the cutting tools are clearly visible.

The ossuaries are variously decorated with incised lines, rosettes and sometimes inscriptions. Ossuary lids are of three types: gabled, flat and convex. We found all three types in our tomb. Often, ossuaries bear scratch marks at one end, extending onto the edge of the lid. These marks served to show how the lid was to be fitted onto the ossuary.

Of the eight ossuaries we found in this tomb, three were *in situ* in loculi in Chamber B; the other five were discovered in Chamber B in the middle of the floor.

We also found a considerable quantity of pottery in the tombs. Because all the pottery was easily identifiable, we were able to date the tomb quite accurately. The entire assemblage can be dated with certainty between the late Hellenistic period (end of the second century B.C., about 180 B.C.) to the Roman destruction of the Second Temple (in 70 A.D.). However, the bulk of the pottery dates to the period following the rise of the Herodian dynasty in 37 B.C. The assemblage included so-called spindle bottles[1] (probably used for aromatic balsam), globular juglets (for oil), oil lamps and even some cooking pots.

The skeletal finds indicate that two generations were buried in this tomb. No doubt this was the tomb of a family of some wealth and perhaps even prominence. The eight ossuaries contained the bones of 17 different people. Each ossuary contained the bones of one to five people. The ossuaries were usually filled to the brim with bones, male and female, adult and child, interred together. One ossuary also held a bouquet of withered flowers.

As we shall see from the inscriptions, at least one member of this family participated in the building of Herod's temple. But despite the wealth and achievement of its members, this family was probably not a happy one. As osteological examination showed that five of the 17 people whose bones were collected in the ossuaries died before reaching the age of seven. By age 37, 75 percent had died. Only two of the 17 lived to be more than 50. One child died of starvation, and one woman was killed when struck on the head by a mace.

And one man in this family had been crucified. He was between 24 and 28 years old, according to our osteologists.

Strange though it may seem, when I excavated the bones of this crucified man, I did not know how he had died. Only when the contents of Ossuary No. 4 from Chamber B of Tomb No. 1 were sent for osteological analysis was it discovered that it contained one three- or four-year-old child and a crucified man—a nail held his heel bones together. The nail was about 7 inches (17-18 cm) long.

Before examining the osteological evidence, I should say a little about crucifixion. Many people erroneously assume that crucifixion was a Roman invention. In fact, Assyrians, Phoenicians and Persians all practiced crucifixion during the first millennium B.C. Crucifixion was introduced in the west from these eastern cultures; it was used

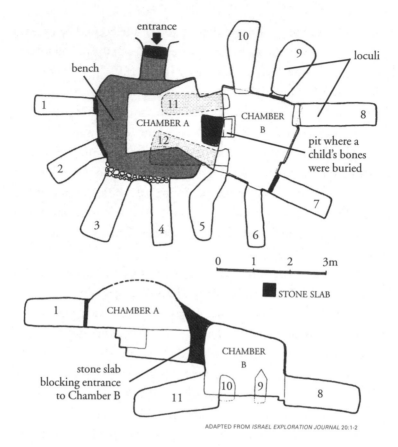

entrance

bench

loculi

1

11

CHAMBER A

12

2

10

9

CHAMBER B

8

pit where a child's bones were buried

7

3

4

5

6

0   1   2   3m

■ STONE SLAB

1

CHAMBER A

stone slab blocking entrance to Chamber B

11

CHAMBER B

10   9   8

The crucifixion victim's remains were found in a typical Jewish burial cave (called Tomb No. 1), shown here in plan and cross-section. The tomb had two chambers (A and B) at different levels; a total of 12 burial niches, or loculi (numbered on the plan), were carved into the chamber walls.

Following a Jewish burial practice common in Jerusalem from about 20 B.C. to 70 A.D., a corpse was initially laid out in a loculus. About a year later, when the body had decomposed, the bones were gathered together in an ossuary, which was then placed in the niche. The excavators of Tomb No. 1 discovered eight ossuaries containing the remains of 17 different people.

only rarely on the Greek mainland, but Greeks in Sicily and southern Italy used it more frequently, probably as a result of their closer contact with Phoenicians and Carthaginians.[2]

During the Hellenistic period, crucifixion became more popular among the Hellenized population of the east. After Alexander died in 323 B.C., crucifixion was frequently employed both by the Seleucids (the rulers of the Syrian half of Alexander's kingdom) and by the Ptolemies (the rulers of the Egyptian half).

Among the Jews crucifixion was anathema. (See Deuteronomy 21:22-23: "If a man is guilty of a capital offense and is put to death, and you impale him on a stake, you must not let his corpse remain on the stake overnight, but you must bury him the same day. For an impaled body is an affront to God: you shall not defile the land that the Lord your God is giving you to possess.")

The traditional method of execution among Jews was stoning. Nevertheless, crucifixion was occasionally employed by Jewish tyrants during the Hasmonean period. Alexander Jannaeus crucified 800 Jews on a single day in 88 B.C.

At the end of the first century B.C., the Romans adopted crucifixion as an official punishment for non-Romans for certain legally limited transgressions. Initially, it was employed not as a method of execution, but only as a punishment. Moreover, only slaves convicted of certain crimes were punished by crucifixion. During this early period, a wooden beam, known as a *furca* or *patibulum* was placed on the slave's neck and bound to his arms. The slave was then required to march through the neighborhood proclaiming his offense. This march was intended as expiation and humiliation. Later, the slave was also stripped and scourged, increasing both the punishment and humiliation. Still later, instead of walking with his arms tied to the wooden beam, the slave was tied to a vertical stake.

Because the main purpose of this practice was to punish, humiliate and frighten disobedient slaves, the practice did not necessarily result in death. Only in later times, probably in the first century B.C., did crucifixion evolve into a method of execution for those convicted of certain crimes.

Initially, crucifixion was known as the punishment of slaves. Later, it was used to punish foreign captives, rebels and fugitives, especially during times of war and rebellion. Captured enemies and rebels were crucified *en masse*. Accounts of the suppression of the revolt of Spartacus in 71 B.C. tell how the Roman army lined the road from Capua to Rome with 6,000 crucified rebels and 6,000 crosses. After King Herod's death triggered a minor rebellion in Judea in 7 A.D., Quintilius Varus, the Roman Legate of Syria, crucified 2,000 Jews in Jerusalem. During Titus's siege of Jerusalem in 70 A.D., Roman troops crucified as many as 500 Jews a day for several months.

In times of war and rebellion, when hundreds and even thousands of people were crucified within a short period, little if any attention was paid to the way crucifixion was carried out. Crosses were haphazardly constructed, and executioners were impressed from the ranks of Roman legionaries.

In peacetime, crucifixions were carried out according to certain rules, by special persons authorized by the Roman courts. Crucifixions took place at specific locations, for example, in particular fields in Rome and on the Golgotha in Jerusalem. Outside of Italy, the Roman procurators alone possessed authority to impose the death penalty. Thus, when a local provincial court prescribed the death penalty, the consent of the Roman procurator had to be obtained to carry out the sentence.

Once a defendant was found guilty and was condemned to be crucified, the execution was supervised by an official known as the *Carnifix Serarum.* From the tribunal hall, the victim was taken outside, stripped, bound to a column and scourged. The scourging was done with either a stick or a *flagellum*, a Roman instrument with a short handle to which several long, thick thongs had been attached. On the ends of the leather thongs were lead or bone tips. Although the number of strokes imposed was not fixed, care was taken not to kill the victim. Following the beating, the horizontal beam was placed upon the condemned man's shoulders, and he began the long, grueling march to the execution site, usually outside the city walls. A soldier at the head of the procession carried the *titulus*, an inscription written on wood, which stated the defendant's name and the crime for which he had been condemned. Later, this *titulus* was fastened to the victim's cross. When the procession arrived at the execution site, a vertical stake was fixed into the ground. Sometimes the victim was attached to the cross only with ropes. In such a case, the *patibulum* or crossbeam, to which the victim's arms were already bound, was simply affixed to the vertical beam; the victim's feet were then bound to the stake with a few turns of the rope.

If the victim was attached by nails, he was laid on the ground, with his shoulders on the crossbeam, which was then raised and fixed on top of the vertical beam. The victim's feet were then nailed down against this vertical stake.

Without any supplementary body support, the victim would die from muscular spasms and asphyxia in a very short time, certainly within two or three hours. Shortly after being raised on the cross, breathing would become difficult; to get his breath, the victim would attempt to draw himself up on his arms. Initially he would be able to hold himself up for 30 to 60 seconds, but this movement would quickly become increasingly difficult. As he became weaker, the victim would be unable to pull himself up and death would ensue within a few hours.

In order to prolong the agony, Roman executioners devised two instruments that would keep the victim alive on the cross for extended periods of time. One, known as a *sedile*, was a small seat attached to the front of the cross, about halfway down. This device provided some support for the victim's body and may explain the phrase used by the Romans, "to sit on the cross." Both Irenaeus and Justin Martyr describe the cross of Jesus as having five extremities rather than four; the fifth was probably the *sedile*. To increase the victim's suffering, the *sedile* was pointed, thus inflicting horrible pain. The second device added to the cross was the *suppedaneum*, or foot support. It was less painful than the *sedile*, but it also prolonged the victim's agony. Ancient historians record many cases in which the victim stayed alive on the cross for two or three or more days with the use of a *suppedaneum*. The church father Origen writes of having seen a crucified man who survived the whole night and the following day. Josephus refers to a case in which three crucified Jews survived on the cross for three days. During the mass crucifixions following the repression of the revolt of Spartacus in Rome, some of the crucified rebels talked to the soldiers for three days.[3]

Using this historical background and the archaeological evidence, it is possible to reconstruct the crucifixion of the man whose bones I excavated at Giv'at ha-Mivtar.

The most dramatic evidence that this young man was crucified was the nail which penetrated his heel bones. But for this nail, we might never have discovered that the young man had died in this way. The nail was preserved only because it hit a hard knot when it was pounded into the olive wood upright of the cross. The olive wood knot was so hard that, as the blows on the nail became heavier, the end of the nail bent and curled. We found a bit of the olive wood (between 1 and 2 cm) on the tip of the nail. This wood had probably been forced out of the knot where the curled nail hooked into it.

When it came time for the dead victim to be removed from the cross, the executioners could not pull out this nail, bent as it was within the cross. The only way to remove the body was to take an ax or hatchet and amputate the feet. Thereafter, the feet, the nail and a plaque of wood that had been fastened between the head of the nail and the feet remained attached to one another as we found them in Ossuary No. 4. Under the head of the nail, the osteological investigators found the remains of this wooden plaque, made of either acacia or pistacia wood. The wood attached to the curled end of the nail that had penetrated the upright of the cross was, by contrast, olive wood.

At first the investigators thought that the bony material penetrated by the nail was only the right heel bone (*calcaneum*). This assumption initially led them to a mistaken conclusion regarding the victim's position on the cross. Further investigation disclosed, however, that the nail had penetrated both heel bones. The left ankle bone (*sustentaculum tali*) was found still attached to the bone mass adjacent to the right ankle bone, which was itself attached to the right heel bone. When first discovered, the two heel bones appeared to be two formless, unequal bony bulges surrounding an iron nail, coated by a thick calcareous crust. But painstaking investigation gradually disclosed the makeup of the bony mass.[4]

A word about the conditions under which the bones in the ossuaries were studied might be appropriate here. The medical team that studied the bones was given only four weeks to conduct their examination before the bones were reburied in a modern ceremony. Certain long-term preservation procedures were therefore impossible, and this precluded certain kinds of measurements and comparative studies. In the case of the crucified man, however, the investigators were given an additional period of time to study the materials, and it was during this period that the detailed conditions described here were discovered.

When removed from the tomb chamber, each of the eight ossuaries was one-third filled with a syrupy fluid. Strangely enough, the considerable moisture in the ossuaries resulted in a peculiar kind of preservation of the packed bones. The bones immersed in the fluid at the bottom of the ossuaries were coated with a limy sediment. As a result, the nailed heel bones were preserved in relatively good condition. Nevertheless, the overall condition of the bones must be described as fragile.

Before they were studied, the bones were first dehydrated and then impregnated with a preservative. Only then could they be measured and photographed.

Despite these limiting conditions, a detailed and very human picture of the crucified man gradually emerged. At 5 feet 6 inches (167 cm) tall, this young man in his mid- to late-twenties stood at about the mean height for Mediterranean people of the time. His limb bones were fine, slender, graceful and harmonious. The muscles that had been attached to his limb bones were lean, pointing to moderate

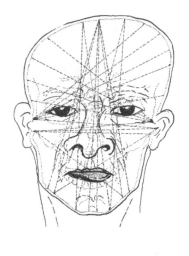 

An artist has reconstructed the victim's appearance based on the skull found in the ossuary. The victim had a cleft palate, a slightly asymmetrical face and a forehead that was flatter on the right side. But hair, beard and moustache might well have disguised these irregularities.

muscular activity, both in childhood and after maturity. Apparently he never engaged in heavy physical labor. We can tell that he had never been seriously injured before his crucifixion, because investigators found no pathological deformations or any traumatic bony lesions. His bones indicated no marks of any disease or nutritional deficiency.

The young man's face, however, was unusual. He had a cleft right palate—a congenital anomaly which was also associated with the congenital absence of the right upper canine tooth and the deformed position of several other teeth. In addition, his facial skeleton was asymmetric, slanting slightly from the one side to the other (plagiocephalic). The eye sockets were at slightly different heights, as were the nasal apertures. There were differences between the left and right branches of the lower jaw bone, and the forehead was more flattened on the right side than on the left. Some of these asymmetries have a direct association with the cleft palate.

The majority of modern medical scholars ascribe a cleft palate (and some associated asymmetries of the face) not to a genetic factor but to a critical change in the manner of life of a pregnant woman in the first two or three weeks of pregnancy. This critical change has frequently been identified as an unexpected deterioration in the woman's diet, in association with psychological stress. Statistically, this malformation occurs more frequently in chronically undernourished and underprivileged families than in the well situated. But some catastrophe could cause sudden stress in the life of a well-to-do woman as well.

Other asymmetries of the facial skeleton may be attributable to disturbances in the final period of pregnancy or difficulties in delivery. Thus, our medical experts conjectured two prenatal crises in the life of this crucified man: one in the first few weeks of his mother's pregnancy and the other a difficult birth.

To help determine the appearance of the face, the team of anatomical experts took 38 anthropological measurements, and determined four cranial indices. The general shape of the facial skeleton, including the forehead, was five-sided. Excluding the forehead, the face was triangular, tapering below eye level. The nasal bones were large, curved, tight in the upper region and coarse in the lower part. The man's nose was curved and his chin robust, altogether a mild-featured facial skeleton.

Despite the prenatal anomalies, the man's face must have been quite pleasant, although some might say that it must have been a bit wild. His defects were doubtless almost imperceptible, hidden by his hair, beard and moustache. His body was proportionate, agreeable and graceful, particularly in motion.

What his life was like, we cannot know. But he seems to have come from a comfortable, if not well-to-do family. One of the ossuaries (not the one containing the crucified man) was inscribed in Aramaic on the side: "Simon, builder of the Temple." Apparently at least one member of the family participated in Herod's lavish rebuilding of the Temple on Jerusalem's Temple Mount. Simon may well have been a master mason or an engineer. Another ossuary was inscribed "Yehonathan the potter."

We may conjecture that during this turbulent period of history, our man was sentenced to crucifixion for some political crime. His remains reveal the horrible manner he died.

From the way in which the bones were attached, we can infer the man's position on the cross. The two heel bones were attached on the adjacent inside (medial) surfaces. The nail went through the right heel bone and then the left. Since the same nail went through both heels, the legs were together, not apart, on the cross.

A study of the two heel bones and the nail that penetrated them at an oblique angle pointed downward and sideways indicates that the feet of the victim were not fastened tightly to the cross. The evidence further suggests that the *sedile* supported only the man's left buttock. This seat both prevented the collapse of the man's body and prolonged his agony.

Given this position on the cross and given the way in which the heel bones were attached to the cross, it seems likely that the knees were bent, or semiflexed, as in the drawing (opposite). This position of the legs was dramatically confirmed by a study of the long bones below the knees, the tibia, or shinbone, and the fibula behind it.

Only the tibia of the crucified man's right leg was available for study. The bone had been brutally fractured into large, sharp slivers. This fracture was clearly produced by a single, strong blow. The left calf bones were lying across the sharp edge of the wooden cross, and the percussion from the blow on the right calf bones passed into the left calf bones, producing a harsh and severing blow to them as well. The left calf bones broke in a straight, sharp-toothed line on the edge of the cross, a line characteristic of a fresh bone fracture. This fracture resulted from the pressure on both sides of the bone—on one side from the direct blow on the right leg and on the other from the resistance of the edge of the cross.

The angle of the fracture indicates that the bones formed an angle of 60 degrees to 65 degrees as they crossed the upright of the cross. This proves that the legs were semiflexed. When we add this evidence to that of the nail and the way in which the heel bones were attached to

Study of the wounds on Yehohan's skeleton enabled osteologists to reconstruct his position on the cross. His arms were nailed above the wrists to the cross-beam. His legs were bent and twisted to one side, and a small sedile, *or seat, supported only his left buttock.*

the cross, we must conclude that the victim's body was forced into a difficult and unnatural position.

The arm bones of the victim reveal the manner in which they were attached to the horizontal bar of the cross. A small scratch was observed on one bone (the radius) of the right forearm, just above the wrist. The scratch was produced by the compression, friction and gliding of an object on the fresh bone. This scratch is the osteological evidence of the penetration of the nail between the two bones of the forearm, the radius and the ulna.

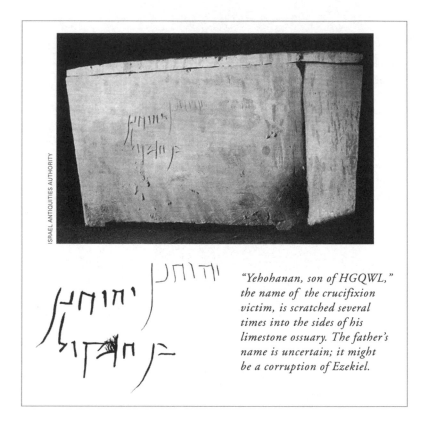

"Yehohanan, son of HGQWL," the name of the crucifixion victim, is scratched several times into the sides of his limestone ossuary. The father's name is uncertain; it might be a corruption of Ezekiel.

Christian iconography usually shows the nails piercing the palms of Jesus' hands. Nailing the palms of the hands is impossible, however, because the weight of the slumping body would have torn the palms in a very short time. The victim would have fallen from the cross while still alive. As the evidence from our crucified man demonstrates, the nails were driven into the victim's arms, just above the wrists, because this part of the arm is sufficiently strong to hold the weight of a slack body.[5]

The position of the crucified body may then be described as follows: The feet were almost parallel, held by the same nail at the heels, with the legs adjacent; the knees were doubled, the right one overlapping the left; the trunk was contorted and seated on a *sedile*; the upper limbs were stretched out, each stabbed by a nail in the forearm.

The victim's broken legs not only provided crucial evidence for the position on the cross, but they also provide evidence for a Palestinian variation of Roman crucifixion—at least as applied to Jews. Normally, the Romans left the crucified person undisturbed to die slowly of sheer physical exhaustion leading to asphyxia. However, Jewish tradition required burial on the day of execution. Therefore, in Palestine the executioner would break the legs of the crucified person in order to hasten his death and thus permit burial before nightfall. This practice, described in the Gospels in reference to the two thieves who were crucified with Jesus (John 32:19), has now been archaeologically confirmed.[6] Since the victim we excavated was a Jew, we may conclude that the executioners broke his legs on purpose in order to accelerate his death and allow his family to bury him before nightfall in accordance with Jewish custom.

We do not know the crime of which our victim was accused. Given the prominence and wealth of the family, it is unlikely that he was a common thief. More likely, he was crucified for political crimes or seditious activities directed against the Roman authorities. Apparently, this Jewish family had two or three sons active in the political, religious and social life of Jerusalem at the end of the Second Temple period. One (Simon) was active in the reconstruction of the Temple. Another (Yehonathan) was a potter. The third son may have been active in anti-Roman political activities, for which he was crucified.

There's something else we know about this victim. We know his name. Scratched on the side of the ossuary containing his bones were the words "Yehohanan, the son of Hagakol."[7]

1. A spindle bottle resembles a cylinder that bulges at its midsection.

2. Diodorus Siculus 24.53.

3. Appian, *Bella Civilia* 1.120.

4. A medical team from the department of anatomy at the Hebrew University Hadassah Medical School, headed by Dr. Nico Haas, made an intensive, if brief, study of the bones.

5. Early Christian artists refrained from drawing scenes of the crucifixion during the first 500 years of Christian history. The earliest Christian representation of the crucifixion dates to the late fifth or early sixth century A.D., that is, about 20 years after crucifixion was legally abolished by the emperor Constantine the Great.

6. In John 19:34, a lance is plunged into Jesus' heart. This was not intended as the death blow but as a post-mortem blow inflicted in order to testify to the victim's death. Only after this testimonial was obtained was the body removed from the cross and handed over to the victim's relatives for burial. The blow to the heart proved beyond doubt that the victim was indeed dead.

7. For further details, see Vassilios Tzaferis, "Jewish Tombs at and near Giv'at ha-Mivtar, Jerusalem," *Israel Exploration Journal* 20:1-2 (1970), pp. 18-32; Nico Haas, "Anthropological Observations on the Skeletal Remains from Giv'at ha-Mivtar," *Israel Exploration Journal* 20:1-2 (1970), pp. 38-59; and Joseph Naveh, "The Ossuary Inscriptions from Giv'at ha-Mivtar," *Israel Exploration Journal* 20:1-2 (1970), pp. 33-37. See also, for a different hypothesis as to the position of Yehohanan on the cross, Yigael Yadin, "Epigraphy and Crucifixion," *Israel Exploration Journal* 23 (1973), pp. 18-22. On the history of crucifixion, see Pierre Barbet, *A Doctor at Calvary* (Image Books, 1963).

CHAPTER SEVEN

NEW ANALYSIS OF THE CRUCIFIED MAN

Hershel Shanks

The preceding chapter dealt with the only remains of a crucified man to be recovered from antiquity. Vassilios Tzaferis, the author of the essay and the excavator of the crucified man, based much of his analysis of the victim's position on the cross and other aspects of the method of crucifixion on the work of a medical team, headed by Nico Haas, from the Hebrew University's Hadassah Medical School. In an article in the *Israel Exploration Journal*, however, Joseph Zias, an anthropologist with the Israel Department of Antiquities, and Eliezer Sekeles, of the Hadassah Medical School, question many of Haas's conclusions concerning the bones of the crucified man.[1] The questions Zias and Sekeles raise affect many of the conclusions about the man's position during crucifixion.

According to Haas, the nail in the crucified man penetrated both his right and left heel bones, piercing the right heel bone (*calcaneum*) first, then the left. Haas found a fragment of bone attached to the right heel that he thought was part of the left heel bone (*sustentaculum tali*). If Haas's analysis is correct, the two heels must have been penetrated by the same nail, and the victim's legs must have been in a closed position.

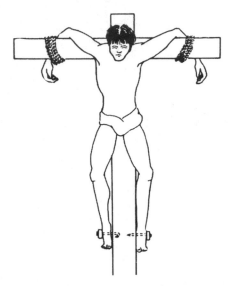

FROM *ISRAEL EXPLORATION JOURNAL* 35:1

A reexamination of the crucified man finds no evidence that nails penetrated the victim's arms; moreover, the nail found in the heel bone was not long enough to have penetrated both feet. Based on this new evidence, the crucifixion victim's pose on the cross has been redrawn to show his legs straddling the cross and his arms tied to the crossbeam with ropes.

But according to the new analysis of the bones just published in the *Israel Exploration Journal*, Haas incorrectly identified the bone fragment attached to the right heel bone. "The shape and structure of this bony fragment is of a long bone; it cannot therefore be the left [heel bone]," say the most recent investigators. Their conclusions are confirmed by X-rays, which reveal the varying density, structure and direction of the bones.

Haas incorrectly assumed that the nail was 7 inches (17-18 cm) long. In fact the total length of the nail from head to tip is only 4.5 inches (11.5 cm). A wooden plaque less than an inch thick (2 cm) had been punctured by the nail before it passed through the right heel bone. After exiting from the bone, the nail penetrated the cross itself and then bent, probably because it hit a knot. As the new investigators observe, given the length of the nail, "There simply was not enough room for both heel bones and a two centimeter wooden plaque to have been pierced by the nail and affixed to the vertical shaft of the cross ... The nail was sufficient for affixing only one heel bone to the cross."

In short, only the right heel bone was penetrated—laterally, or sidewise—by the nail. Accordingly, the victim's position on the cross must have been different from that portrayed by Haas.

The new investigators also dispute Haas's conclusion that a scratch on the bone of the right forearm (*radius*) of the victim, just above the wrist, represents the penetration of a nail between the two bones of the forearm. According to Zias and Sekeles, such scratches and indentations are commonly found on ancient skeletal material, including on the right leg bone (*fibula*) of this man. Such scratches and indentations have nothing to do with crucifixion.

How then was the crucified man attached to the cross? As the new investigators observe:

> The literary sources for the Roman period contain numerous descriptions of crucifixion but few exact details as to how the condemned were affixed to the cross. Unfortunately, the direct physical evidence here is also limited to one right calcaneum (heel bone) pierced by an 11.5 cm iron nail with traces of wood at both ends.

According to the literary sources, those condemned to crucifixion never carried the complete cross, despite the common belief to the contrary and despite the many modern reenactments of Jesus' walk to Golgotha. Instead, only the crossbar was carried, while the upright was set in a permanent place, where it was used for subsequent executions. As the first-century Jewish historian Josephus noted, wood was so scarce in Jerusalem during the first century A.D. that the Romans were forced to travel 10 miles from Jerusalem to secure timber for their siege machinery.

Zias and Sekeles write:

> One can reasonably assume that the scarcity of wood may have been
> expressed in the economics of crucifixion in that the crossbar as well
> as the upright would be used repeatedly. Thus the lack of traumatic
> injury to the forearm and metacarpals of the hand seems to suggest
> that the arms of the condemned were tied rather than nailed to the
> cross. There is ample literary and artistic evidence for the use of
> ropes rather than nails to secure the condemned to the cross.

According to Zias and Sekeles, the victim's legs straddled the vertical shaft of the cross, one leg on either side, with the nails penetrating the heel bones. The plaque or plate under the head of the nail, they say, was intended to secure the nail and prevent the condemned man from pulling his feet free.

As Haas correctly suggested, the nail probably hit a knot which bent the nail. However Zias and Sekeles offer a different reconstruction of the removal of the dead man from the cross:

> Once the body was removed from the cross, albeit with some diffi-
> culty in removing the right leg, the condemned man's family would
> now find it impossible to remove the bent nail without completely
> destroying the heel bone. This reluctance to inflict further damage
> to the heel led [to his burial with the nail still in his bone, and this
> in turn led] to the eventual discovery of the crucifixion.

Whether the victim's arms were tied, rather than nailed to the cross is irrelevant to the manner of his dying, as Zias and Sekeles point out:

> Death by crucifixion was the result of the manner in which the con-
> demned hung from the cross and not the traumatic injury caused by
> nailing. Hanging from the cross resulted in a painful process of
> asphyxiation, in which the two sets of muscles used for breathing, the

intercostal [chest] muscles and the diaphragm, became progressively weakened. In time, the condemned man expired, due to the inability to continue breathing properly.

1. Joseph Zias and Eliezer Sekeles, "The Crucified Man from Giv'at ha-Mitvar: A Reappraisal," *Israel Exploration Journal* 35:1 (1985), pp. 22-27.

Zias and Sekeles also note a number of other errors in Haas's report:

The victim's legs were not broken as a final *coup de grâce.* The break so identified by Haas was post-mortem.

The victim did not have a cleft palate. The upper right canine was not missing, despite Haas's report to the contrary.

The wood from which the plaque under the nail head was made was olive wood, not acacia or pistacia, as Haas suggested.

The wood fragments attached to the end of the nail were too minute to be analyzed. Haas suggested the vertical shaft of the cross was olive wood. This is possible, but unlikely.

CHAPTER EIGHT

WHERE WAS JESUS BURIED?

Dan Bahat

Since 1960, the Armenian, the Greek and the Latin religious com-munities that are responsible for the care of the Holy Sepulchre Church in Jerusalem have been engaged in a joint restoration project of one of the most fascinating—and complex—buildings in the world.

In connection with the restoration, they have undertaken exten-sive archaeological work in an effort to establish the history of the building and of the site on which it rests. Thirteen trenches were excavated primarily to check the stability of Crusader structures, but these trenches were also used for archaeological excavations. Stripping plaster from the walls revealed structures from earlier peri-ods. A new, modern drainage system was put in place, but the work itself was also used for archaeological research. Elsewhere, soundings were made for purely archaeological purposes.

The results of all this excavation and research have now been pub-lished in a three-volume final report by Virgilio C. Corbo, professor of archaeology at the Studium Biblicum Franciscanum in Jerusalem.[1] Father Corbo has been intimately involved in this archaeological work for more than 20 years, and no one is better able to report on the results than he.[2]

Signs of ancient quarrying were found everywhere beneath the Church of the Holy Sepulchre. Here we see the outlines of partially cut stone blocks that were never fully removed from the quarry. The stone is a high-quality limestone called meleke. *The area served as a quarry from at least the seventh century B.C. until the first century B.C., when it was covered with arable soil and transformed into a garden or orchard.*

Although the text itself (Volume I) is in Italian, there is a 16-page English summary by Stanislao Loffreda. Father Loffreda has also translated into English the captions to the archaeological drawings and reconstructions (Volume II) and the archaeological photographs (Volume III). So this handsome set will be accessible to the English-speaking world as well as to those who read Italian.

During the late Judean monarchy, beginning in the eighth or seventh century B.C., the area where the Holy Sepulchre Church is now located was a large limestone quarry. The city itself lay to the southeast and expanded first westward and then northward only at a later date. A high quality type of limestone called *meleke* has been found wherever the excavations in the church reached bedrock. Traces of the quarry have been found not only in the church area, but also in excavations conducted by Kathleen Kenyon in the 1960s and 1970s, in the nearby Muristan enclave of the Christian quarter, and by Ute Lux, in the nearby Church of the Redeemer. This *meleke* stone was chiseled out in squarish blocks for building purposes. The artificially shaped and cut rock surface that remains reveals to the archaeologist that the area was originally a quarry.

Sometimes the workers left partially cut ashlars still attached to the bedrock. In one area (east of St. Helena's Chapel in the Holy Sepulchre Church), the quarry was over 40 feet deep. The earth and ash that filled the quarry contained Iron Age II pottery, from about the seventh century B.C.; so the quarry can be securely dated.[3]

According to Father Corbo, this quarry continued to be used until the first century B.C. At that time, the quarry was filled, and a layer of reddish-brown soil mixed with stone flakes from the ancient quarry was spread over it. The quarry became a garden or orchard, where cereals, fig trees, carob trees and olive trees grew. For Father Corbo, the layer of arable soil above the quarry is evidence of the garden.[4] At this same time, the quarry-garden also became a cemetery. At least four tombs dating from this period have been found.

The first is the tomb traditionally known as the tomb of Nicodemus and Joseph of Arimathea (No. 28 in Corbo's list). The Gospel accounts (John 19:38-41; Luke 23:50-53; Matthew 27:57-61) report that Joseph took Jesus' body down from the cross; Nicodemus brought myrrh and aloes and, together, he and Joseph wrapped Jesus' body in linen and buried him in a garden in Joseph's newly cut, rock-hewn tomb.

The tomb traditionally attributed to Nicodemus and Joseph of Arimathea is a typical *kokh* (plural, *kokhim*) of the first century. *Kokhim* (also called loculi) are long, narrow recesses in a burial cave where either a coffin or the body of the deceased could be laid. Sometimes ossuaries (boxes of bones collected about a year after the original burial) were placed in *kokhim*.

In the course of restoration work in the Holy Sepulchre Church a hitherto unknown passage to this tomb was found beneath the rotunda.

Another type of tomb, known as an *arcosolium* (plural *arcosolia*), was also common in this period. An *arcosolium* is a shallow, rock-hewn coffin cut lengthwise in the side of a burial cave. It has an arch-shaped top over the recess, from which its name is derived. The so-called tomb of Jesus is composed of an antechamber and a rock-cut *arcosolium*.

HERSHEL SHANKS

Beneath the north wall of the rotunda lies a tomb traditionally attributed to Nicodemus and Joseph of Arimathea. According to the Gospels, Joseph took Jesus' body down from the cross and, with Nicodemus's assistance, buried him in his own newly cut tomb. A typical first-century tomb, it has two long recesses (called loculi or, in Hebrew, kokhim) *where bodies could be placed.*

Unfortunately, centuries of pilgrims have completely deformed this tomb by pecking and chipping away bits of rock as souvenirs or for their reliquaries. Today the tomb is completely covered with later masonry, but enough is known to identify it as an *arcosolium* from about the turn of the era.

A third, much larger tomb, probably of the *kokh* type, was found in front of the church (in the parvis). This tomb was greatly enlarged in Constantine's time and was used as a cistern. Very little remains of it, but Corbo's study reveals its original function as a tomb.

Finally, although not mentioned by Corbo, in the late 19th century another tomb of the *kokh* type was found in the church area under the Coptic convent.[5]

Obviously many other tombs that existed in the area were destroyed by later structures. But the evidence seems clear that at the turn of the era, this area was a large burial ground.

The tomb in front of the church was actually cut into the rock of what is traditionally regarded as the hill of Golgotha, where Jesus was crucified. It is possible that the rocky outcrop of Golgotha was a *nefesh*, or memorial monument.[6] However, this hypothesis needs more study before it can be advanced with any confidence.

The next period for which we have archaeological evidence in the Holy Sepulchre Church is from the period of the Roman emperor Hadrian. In 70 A.D. the Romans crushed the First Jewish Revolt; at that time they destroyed Jerusalem and burned the Temple. Less than 70 years later, in 132 A.D., the Jews again revolted, this time under the leadership of Rabbi Akivah and Bar-Kokhba. It took the Romans three years to suppress the Second Jewish Revolt. This time, however, the victorious Roman emperor Hadrian banned Jews from Jerusalem and trenched around it a *pomerium*, a furrow plowed by the founder of a new city to mark its confines. To remove every trace of its Jewish past, Hadrian rebuilt Jerusalem as a Roman city named Aelia Capitolina. (For the same reason, he also changed the name of the country from Judea to Palaestina or Palestine.)

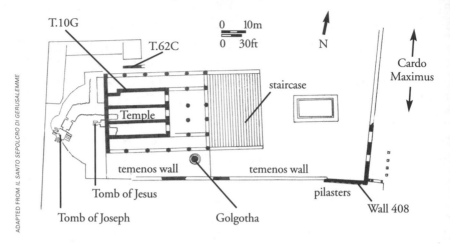

When Constantine commissioned the Church of the Holy Sepulchre in the fourth century, he first had to tear down a pagan temple built on the site 200 years earlier by Hadrian. This reconstruction of the temple plan, by Virgilio Corbo, shows a tripartite rectangular structure entered from the east. A columned portico surrounded the temple on three sides. According to Corbo, the temple was dedicated to Venus, Minerva and Jupiter. The gods' statues stood inside, in three niches. The temple rested on a massive platform supported by a retaining wall. An extant portion of the wall (lower right, called Wall 408) is visible in the photo, opposite.

On the site of the former seventh-century B.C. quarry and first-century B.C. orchard-garden and cemetery, where the Holy Sepulchre Church would later be built, Hadrian constructed a gigantic raised platform—that is, a nearly rectangular retaining wall (called the *temenos* wall) filled with earth. On top of the platform, he built a smaller raised podium, and on top of the podium, he built a temple. Although the remains of the Hadrianic retaining wall are scant, its existence is clear.

Because the area had been dug as a quarry and because it had also been honeycombed with tombs and was left with depressions and protrusions of uncut rock, the building of this platform was necessary to create a level construction site.

Many of the ashlars (chiseled building stones) used by Hadrian for the retaining wall of the platform were actually old Herodian ashlars—

left from the Roman destruction of Jerusalem and of Herod's Temple in 70 A.D. They are identical in size and facing to the Herodian ashlars in the retaining wall of the Temple Mount. Hadrian's wall therefore looked like a Herodian wall—much like the famous Western Wall of the Temple Mount, which is, even today, a focus of Jewish reverence.

Although not mentioned by Corbo, the upper part of Hadrian's retaining wall even had slightly protruding pilasters or engaged pillars along the outer face, thereby creating the appearance of regularly spaced recesses. In this way, too, the Hadrianic enclosure duplicated

Large stones from the retaining wall that supported Hadrian's temple platform were found in excavations east of the Church of the Holy Sepulchre. In this photo, the stones make up the first few courses in the wall above the stairs. Hadrian likely borrowed these stones from the ruins of the Temple Mount. The size and shape (with narrow margins and a large flat central boss) is typical of the stones used by Herod when he constructed the Temple Mount.

Note how the wall juts out. The upper reaches of Hadrian's retaining wall apparently had pilasters, or engaged columns, protruding from the wall. This design is also borrowed from Herod's Temple Mount wall, which had pilasters part way up the wall.

the Herodian Temple Mount enclosure, although unfortunately the latter did not survive to a height that included these pilasters, except in traces. This style can be seen today, however, in the Herodian wall enclosing the traditional tomb of the patriarchs (the cave of Machpelah) at Hebron.

That Hadrian appears to have deliberately attempted to duplicate the Herodian enclosure of the Temple Mount has special significance. Instead of a temple to Yahweh, however, Hadrian built on his raised enclosure an elaborate temple to the goddess of love, Venus/Aphrodite.

Corbo refers to Hadrian's temple as Capitolium, that is, as being dedicated to Jupiter the Capitoline. For this, he relies on the fifth-century testimony of Jerome, who mentions a Jerusalem temple dedicated to Jupiter. However, Eusebius in the fourth century tells us Hadrian's temple at this site was dedicated to Venus/Aphrodite. There is no reason for Corbo to prefer Jupiter over Venus/Aphrodite, especially because Dio Cassius in the third century fixes the site of the temple of Jupiter on the site of the former Jewish Temple, that is, on the Temple Mount. That is the temple Jerome is referring to. A number of other ancient writers from the fifth century on refer to a temple of Venus/Aphrodite on the site where the Church of the Holy Sepulchre was later built.

To support his attribution to Jupiter, Corbo claims to have found in the rotunda of the church two fragments from a triple cella that would have accommodated statues of the Capitoline triad: Venus, Minerva and Jupiter. There is no basis, however, for suggesting that these fragmentary remains are part of a triple cella—or even that they are part of the pagan temple itself. As so often in this report, Corbo's assertion as to the date of walls is merely that—pure assertion. No evidence is given.

Parts of Hadrian's enclosure wall have survived. According to Corbo, fragments of other walls, found in cisterns and in what was the first-century B.C. garden, belonged to the substructure of Hadrian's temple. But for this, as before, we must rely solely on Corbo's assertion. He presents no evidence on which his conclusions can be tested. In any event, none of the visible parts of Hadrian's temple has been discovered. As we know from historical sources, it was razed to the ground by Constantine, so there is no hope of recovering it. Likewise, the small podium on which the temple sat, on top of the enclosure-platform, has also vanished without a trace.

Corbo's reconstruction of the Hadrianic temple is thus completely speculative—and unsatisfactory. In the first place, he assumes it was a three-niche structure pursuant to his mistaken theory that it was dedicated to Jupiter the Capitoline rather than Venus/Aphrodite.[7] But, in any event, there is no known parallel to Corbo's plan.[8]

Queen Helena, Constantine's mother, was shown the site on her visit to Jerusalem in 326 A.D. We do not know the condition of the site at this time. Perhaps the pagan temple constructed by Hadrian was already in ruins—destroyed by zealous Christians.

After Queen Helena's visit, the Christian community proceeded to remove whatever was left of the Hadrianic temple, as well as the Hadrianic enclosure and the fill it contained. For the Christian community, this fill, intended by Hadrian to create a level surface for building, represented Hadrian's attempt to obliterate forever not only Jesus' tomb, but the adjacent rock of Golgotha where he had been crucified.

According to literary sources[9] Constantine built a rotunda around Jesus' tomb. In front of the rotunda was the site of the crucifixion (Golgotha or Calvary), in what is referred to in ancient literary sources as the Holy Garden. On the other side of the garden, Constantine built a long church in the shape of a basilica, consisting of a nave and side aisles separated from the nave by rows of columns. Here the faithful could offer prayers. Between the rotunda and the basilica lay the hill of Golgotha (see plan, p. 126).

Was the Constantinian rotunda actually built over the true site of Jesus' burial?

Although we can never be certain it seems very likely it was.

As we have seen, the site was a turn-of-the-era cemetery. The cemetery, including Jesus' tomb, had itself been buried for nearly 300

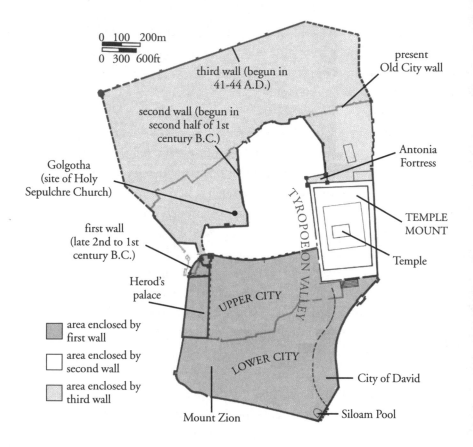

0 100 200m
0 300 600ft

third wall (begun in
41-44 A.D.)

present
Old City wall

second wall (begun in
second half of 1st
century B.C.)

Antonia
Fortress

Golgotha
(site of Holy
Sepulchre Church)

TEMPLE
MOUNT

first wall
(late 2nd to 1st
century B.C.)

Temple

Herod's
palace

TYROPOEON VALLEY

UPPER CITY

area enclosed by
first wall

area enclosed by
second wall

LOWER CITY

City of David

area enclosed by
third wall

Mount Zion

Siloam Pool

Crucifixions and burials took place outside city walls in ancient times. Thus, for the site where the Church of the Holy Sepulchre stood to be biblical Golgotha, it had to have been outside the city walls in Jesus' time. As shown in this map, for most of the first century B.C., Jerusalem was limited to the Temple Mount, the City of David and Mount Zion. In the late first century B.C., the area just west and northwest of the Temple Mount was incorporated into the city; Golgotha apparently remained just outside this second wall (the archaeological evidence for this second wall is limited, however, leading to several different interpretations of its line, including that of Jerome Murphy-O'Connor in the map on p. 75). This was the case when Jesus was crucified; the Gospel of John describes the location as "near the city" (John 19:20). But about ten years later, in 41 to 44 A.D., Herod Agrippa built the so-called third wall. Although scholars dispute the precise line of this wall, all agree that Golgotha was inside it. Today, the Holy Sepulchre and Golgotha lie within the Old City wall.

years. The fact that it had indeed been a cemetery, and that this memory of Jesus' tomb survived despite Hadrian's burial of it with his enclosure fill, speaks to the authenticity of the site. Moreover, the fact that the Christian community in Jerusalem was never dispersed during this period and that its succession of bishops was never interrupted supports the accuracy of the preserved memory that Jesus had been crucified and buried here.

Perhaps the strongest argument in favor of the authenticity of the site, however, is that it must have been regarded as such an unlikely site when pointed out to Constantine's mother Queen Helena in the fourth century. Then, as now, the site of what was to be the Church of the Holy Sepulchre was in a crowded urban location that must have seemed as strange to a fourth-century pilgrim as it does to a modern one. But we now know that its location perfectly fits first-century conditions.

By the fourth century this site had long been enclosed within the city walls. The wall enclosing this part of the city (referred to by Josephus as the Third Wall) had been built by Herod Agrippa, the local ruler who governed Judea between 41 and 44 A.D. Thus, this wall was built very soon after Jesus' crucifixion—not more than 10 to 15 years afterward. And that is the crucial point.

When Jesus was buried in about 30 A.D., this area was outside the city, in a garden, Corbo tells us, certainly in a cemetery of that time. These are the facts revealed by modern archaeology. Yet who could have known this in 325 A.D. if the memory of Jesus' burial had not been accurately preserved?

The Gospels tell us that Jesus was buried "near the city" (John 19:20); the site we are considering was then just outside the city, the city wall being only about 500 feet to the south and 350 feet to the east. We are also told the site was in a garden (John 19:41), which is at the very least consistent with the evidence we have of the condition of the site in the first century.

We may not be absolutely certain that the site of the Holy Sepulchre Church is the site of Jesus' burial, but we certainly have no

Constantine's Church

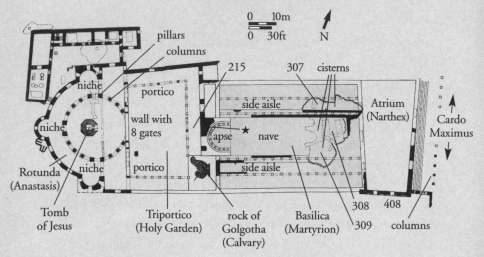

0   10m

0   30ft   N

pillars

columns

215   307 cisterns

niche

portico

side aisle

Atrium
(Narthex)

niche

wall with
8 gates

apse   ★ nave

Cardo
Maximus

niche

portico

side aisle

Rotunda
(Anastasis)

Tomb
of Jesus

Triportico
(Holy Garden)

rock of
Golgotha
(Calvary)

Basilica
(Martyrion)

308 408

309 columns

In the plan (above) of Constantine's fourth-century Church of the Holy Sepulchre, black areas indicate extant remains; dotted structures were not found but are assumed to have existed. The church was approached from the Cardo Maximus, the city's major north-south thoroughfare. A series of steps led up to an atrium, where three doors led into the basilica. The nave was flanked by two rows of aisles separated by columns. Three cisterns (307, 308 and 309) located beneath the eastern end of the basilica would be turned into chapels in the Crusader period. A porticoed Holy Garden lay just west of the basilica. In the southeast corner of the garden is the rock of Golgotha, or Calvary. Eight gates led from the garden into the rotunda, which had three niches in its outer wall. Inside the rotunda, columns and pillars surrounded Jesus' tomb.

The Holy Sepulchre was destroyed by the Fatimid Caliph, El Khakim, in 1009, and then rebuilt by Constantine IX Monomachus in 1048 along the top right plan. (Here, too, black areas indicate extant remains.) The rotunda was reconstructed with a fourth niche on the east side. The Holy Garden was retained, but the Constantinian basilica almost disappeared. In its place, just east of the garden, were three chapels, known only from literary sources. Another set of three chapels was built south of the rotunda, and a single chapel to the north. The entrance to the complex was in the south, through the Holy Garden. The modern entrance is in the same place.

The basic plan of the church today is that of the 12th-century Crusader church (lower right). The rotunda encloses the tomb of Jesus as before, but now, for the first time, the rock of Golgotha is also inside the church. On the site of the Holy Garden, the Crusaders constructed a basilica with a nave, transept and high altar. The Crusaders also constructed three chapels near the cisterns (307-309) that lay beneath Constantine's original basilica. The chapels are dedicated to St. Helena, the True Cross and St. Vartan.

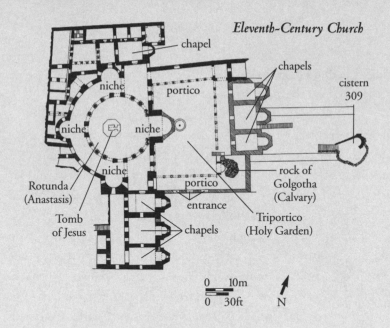

Eleventh-Century Church

chapel

niche

portico

chapels

cistern 309

niche

niche

niche

Rotunda (Anastasis)

portico

rock of Golgotha (Calvary)

Tomb of Jesus

entrance

chapels

Triportico (Holy Garden)

0 — 10m
0 — 30ft

N

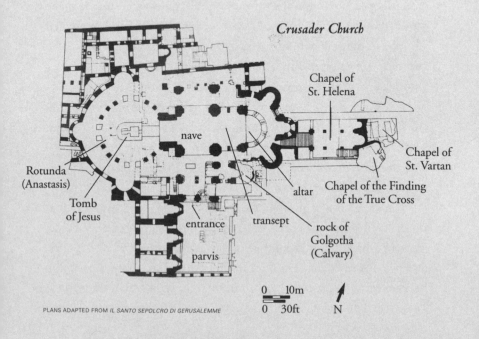

Crusader Church

Chapel of St. Helena

nave

Chapel of St. Vartan

Rotunda (Anastasis)

Chapel of the Finding of the True Cross

Tomb of Jesus

altar

entrance

transept

rock of Golgotha (Calvary)

parvis

PLANS ADAPTED FROM *IL SANTO SEPOLCRO DI GERUSALEMME*

0 — 10m
0 — 30ft

N

other site that can lay a claim nearly as weighty, and we really have no reason to reject the authenticity of the site.

The basilica Constantine built in front of the tomb was typical of its time. It consisted of a center nave and aisles on either side of the nave separated from the nave by rows of columns. At the far end of the nave was a single apse. Unfortunately hardly a trace of Constantine's basilica church remains. From the sections of wall discovered, we can only confirm its location and former existence.

Behind (west of) Constantine's basilica was a large open garden on the other side of which, in the rotunda, stood the tomb of Jesus. The apse of the basilica faced the tomb. Two principal scholars involved in the restoration disagree as to when the tomb was enclosed by a large imposing rotunda. Corbo takes one view; Father Charles Coüasnon takes another. Coüasnon, who died in 1976, had been the architect of the Latin community connected with the restoration work. In 1974 he published a preliminary report of the excavations, entitled *The Church of the Holy Sepulchre in Jerusalem* (London: Oxford University Press). According to Coüasnon the tomb was set in an isolated square niche annexed to the Holy Garden. Coüasnon believed the tomb remained exposed to the open air until after Constantine's death, at which time the rotunda was built around it, leaving the Holy Garden between the rotunda and the back of Constantine's basilica church.

This view is rejected by Corbo, who is probably correct. According to Corbo, the rotunda was part of the original design. Unfortunately, from the nature of Corbo's excavation methodology and the limited archaeological evidence in this report, it is impossible to check his dating of the walls.

There is one argument Corbo fails to make, however, that might well support his position; many temples to goddesses (like Venus/Aphrodite) are round, in the form of rotundas. If it is true, as Eusebius says, that Hadrian built a temple to Venus/Aphrodite here, it was quite probably a round temple, rather than the rectangular temple Corbo has reconstructed. The Christian rotunda may

The rotunda, often called the Anastasis (Greek, "Resurrection") is the focal point of the Church of the Holy Sepulchre. The pillars and columns of the rotunda enclose the reconstructed tomb of Jesus, shown in this fish-eye photo.

well have been inspired by this pagan rotunda. (The phenomenon of a holy site from one religion being maintained as holy by subsequent religions was a common one throughout the ancient world.) If the architecture of Hadrian's pagan rotunda inspired the rotunda around Jesus' tomb, it is more likely that the later rotunda was built by Constantine himself, not by a later ruler who would not have known the pagan rotunda.

Two original columns of the rotunda built around Jesus' tomb have been preserved. Father Coüasnon suggested they were two halves of what was once a single, tall column. According to Coüasnon, this column previously served in the portico of the Hadrianic temple; the two halves were later reused in the rotunda. In this, he is probably correct.

On the side of the niche that marked Jesus' tomb, a drain had been cut in the rock, apparently to allow the flow of rain water from the tomb. This might indicate that at least for some time the tomb stood in the open air. How long we cannot know.

In any event, a rotunda was soon built around the tomb where the current reconstructed tomb—the focus of the present church—now stands (see photo, p. 129). This rotunda is often referred to, both now and in historical records, as the Anastasis (meaning "Resurrection").

Between the rotunda and the basilica church was the Holy Garden. According to Coüasnon, the Holy Garden was enclosed on all four sides by a portico set on a row of columns, thus creating a colonnaded, rectangular courtyard. Beyond the porticoed court-yard, on the rotunda side, was a wall with eight gates that led to the rotunda. Corbo, on the other hand, reconstructs columns on only three sides. (Thus, he calls the garden courtyard the triportico.) Corbo would omit the portico on the rotunda side, adjacent to the eight-gated wall. He is probably right.

Thus the complex of the Church of the Holy Sepulchre stood until the Persian invasion of 614 A.D. At that time it was damaged by fire, but not, as once supposed, totally destroyed. When the Persians conquered Jerusalem, they destroyed many of its churches, but not the Holy Sepulchre.

The situation was different, however, in 1009 A.D. On the order of the Fatimid Caliph of Cairo, El Khakim, the entire church com-plex—the basilica, the rotunda, the tomb inside the rotunda, and the portico between the rotunda and the basilica—was badly damaged and almost completely destroyed.

The basilica was gone forever, razed to the ground. Only the 1968 discovery of the foundation of the western apse of the basilica allows its placement to be fixed with certainty (although previous recon-structions had fixed its location correctly).

The rotunda, however, was preserved to a height of about 5 feet. Between 1042 and 1048 the Byzantine emperor Constantine IX

Monomachus attempted to restore the complex. He was most successful with the rotunda, which was restored with only slight change (see plan, p. 127). Where the Constantinian rotunda had three niches on three sides, Monomachus added a fourth. This new niche was on the east side, the direction of prayer in most churches. The new niche was the largest of the niches and was no doubt the focus of prayer in the rotunda.

In front of the rotunda, Monomachus retained the open garden. One of the old colonnades (the northern one) was rebuilt by him and has been preserved to the present time, thus enabling us to study the character of Monomachus's restoration.

Instead of a basilica, Monomachus built three groups of chapels. One group, consisting of three chapels, abutted the old baptistery; a second group, also consisting of three chapels, was built near the site of the apse of the destroyed basilica (this group is known from historical documentation only); and the third consisted of a chapel north of the rotunda.

In the course of his reconstruction, Monomachus discovered a cistern where, according to tradition, Queen Helena had discovered the True Cross. Corbo believes, probably correctly, that this tradition originated only in the 11th century. (On archaeological grounds, the cistern dates to the 11th or 12th century.) Moreover, nothing was built to commemorate Helena's supposed discovery of the True Cross here until even later in the Crusader period. Coüasnon, on the other hand, believed the tradition that Queen Helena found the True Cross here dated from Constantinian times. According to Coüasnon, Constantine built a small crypt in the cave-cistern. Coüasnon recognized, however, that the current Chapel of St. Helena dates to the Crusader period. At that time, the famous Chapel of St. Helena, which is a focus of interest even today, was constructed partially in and partially adjacent to the cistern.

The Crusaders, who ruled Jerusalem from 1099 to 1187, also rebuilt the church, essentially in the form we know it today (see plan, p. 127). The rotunda (or Anastasis) enclosing the tomb was maintained as the focus of the new structure. In the area of the porticoed

FROM IL SANTO SEPOLCRO DI GERUSALEMME

Delicate stone carving, much of it now lost, decorated the Crusader entrance.

garden in front of the rotunda, the Crusaders built a nave with a transept, forming a cross, and installed a high altar.

The traditional rock of Golgotha, where Jesus had been crucified, was enclosed—for the first time—in this church. In Hadrian's time, the rock of Golgotha had protruded above the Hadrianic enclosure-platform. According to Jerome, a statue of Venus/Aphrodite was set on top of the protruding rock. This statue was no doubt removed by Christians who venerated the rock. When Constantine built his basilica, the rock was squared in order to fit it into a chapel in the southeast corner of the Holy Garden. As noted, in the Crusader church the rock was enclosed in a chapel within the church itself. The floor level of this chapel, where the rock may still be seen, is almost at the height of the top of the rock. Because of this, a lower chapel, named for Adam, was installed to expose the lower part of the rock. This lower chapel served as a burial chapel in the 12th century for the Crusader kings of the Later Kingdom of Jerusalem. These tombs were removed after the great fire of 1808.

Father Corbo's book may well be the last word on the Church of the Holy Sepulchre for a long time to come. Despite its monumental nature, it is, alas, not beyond criticism. It is in no sense an archaeological report, despite the reference in the title of Corbo's book to the "archaeological aspects" of the site. There is not even a discussion of the stylistic development of the building—the rotunda, for example, or

ISRAEL MINISTRY OF TOURISM

Modern pilgrims to the Church of the Holy Sepulchre enter through this door in the façade added during the Crusader period. The bell tower at left is an even later Crusader addition. The rotunda that marks the tomb of Jesus is only halfway visible behind the tower.

the Crusader church as part of the development of the Romanesque European church. Almost no finds are described and it is impossible to understand from Father Corbo's plates and text why a particular wall is ascribed to one period or another. This is a pity. Precise descriptions of these finds and their *loci* (findspots) would have increased our knowledge significantly, not only with respect to the history of the church, but also with respect to the study of medieval pottery, coins and other artifacts. It is also important that scholars be able to check for themselves the attribution of walls and other architectural elements.[10]

From the archaeological point of view, the book under review is definitely unsatisfactory. Nevertheless, no student of this great structure can afford to be without these volumes.

1. Virgilio C. Corbo, *Il Santo Sepolcro di Gerusalemme: Aspetti archeologici dalle origini al periodo crociato*, parts I-III (Jerusalem: Franciscan Printing Press, 1981-1982).

2. In 1960 he was appointed archaeologist for the Latin community on the project; in 1963, for the Greek and Armenian communities as well.

3. See Magen Broshi, "Recent Excavations in the Church of the Holy Sepulchre," *Qadmoniot* 10:1 (1977), pp. 30ff (in Hebrew). More recently, see Magen Broshi and Gabriel Barkay, "Excavations in the Chapel of St. Vartan in the Holy Sepulchre," *Israel Exploration Journal* 35:2-3 (1985), pp. 108ff.

4. Broshi and Barkay (see previous note) do not mention this layer of arable soil; instead they found an Iron Age II floor of beaten earth above the quarry fill. Based on this floor and the large quantities of Iron Age II pottery found below, in and above this floor, they conclude this area was residential from the late eighth century to the Babylonian destruction of Jerusalem. They date the quarry mainly to the ninth and eighth centuries B.C. before the city expanded into this extramural area in the late eighth century. Corbo contends that this floor cannot be dated to Iron Age II.

5. Conrad Schick, "Notes from Jerusalem," *Palestine Exploration Fund Quarterly Statement* (1887), pp. 156-170.

6. *Nefesh* literally means "soul." In rabbinic literature, it also refers to a monument constructed over a grave as a memorial to the deceased. In contemporaneous Greek inscriptions, the equivalent term is *stele*.

7. Moreover, in the reconstruction itself, Wall T 62 C has no function. Wall T 10 G with two angles makes no sense at all.

8. If Corbo intended as his model the Maison Carée in Nîmes, France, or the Temple of Fortuna in Rome, both of which were contemporaneous with Hadrian's temple on the site of the future Church of the Holy Sepulchre, Corbo failed to follow his models. The staircase should not occupy the whole breadth of the structure; behind the six interior columns there should be two additional columns enclosed in two *antae*,

armlike walls that extend from the main walls of the structure; and the lateral columns should not be freestanding, but only half columns attached to the side walls.

9. Especially Eusebius, *Life of Constantine* (Palestine Pilgrims Texts Society, 1891), vol. 1, pp. 1-12.

10. In photograph No. 207, for example, we are shown a fragment attributed by Corbo to Baldwin V's tombstone, but it is almost impossible to understand where it was found, as only a general location is mentioned (see also photos 24, 25 and 204). Unlike many archaeological reports, Corbo gives us no *loci* index. Thus anyone who wishes to study thoroughly a particular *locus* and its contents, location and attribution to a particular period is completely stymied.

Corbo has provided no plans superimposing various periods. There is no grid where one can reconstruct the continuity of the various walls and their relation to one another. One must rely solely on the author's assumptions. He apparently justifies his attribution of walls and floors to particular periods principally on his concept of the shape of the church in a particular period.

There are other shortcomings: The meaning of the shading in some of the plates is not always given in the legend, so it is not always clear what the shading refers to. The location of the sections is not always shown on the plans, so, for example in plate 52, it is not clear where the section of the cistern in plate 53 is located.

No heights are marked on the plans. Thus, for example, when we examine the author's extremely important reconstruction of the pagan structure that preceded the rotunda, we cannot know whether a certain wall is a retaining wall, which it probably was, or a freestanding wall.

Further Reading

A selection of related articles published in *Bible Review (BR)* and *Biblical Archaeology Review (BAR)*.

The Last Supper
Baruch M. Bokser, "Was the Last Supper a Passover Seder?" BR, Summer 1987. Jonathan Klawans, "Was Jesus' Last Supper a Seder?" BR, October 2001. Bargil Pixner, "Church of the Apostles Found on Mt. Zion," BAR, May/June 1990.

Death of Jesus
David Ulansey, "Heavens Torn Open—Mark's Powerful Metaphor Explained," BR, August 1991. Frederick T. Zugibe, "Two Questions About Crucifixion: Does the Victim Die of Asphyxiation? Would Nails in the Hands Hold the Weight of the Body?" BR, April 1989.

The Burial of Jesus
Gabriel Barkay, "The Garden Tomb—Was Jesus Buried Here?" BAR, March/April 1986. Shulamit Eisenstadt, "Jesus' Tomb Depicted on a Byzantine Gold Ring from Jerusalem," BAR, March/April 1987. Amos Kloner, "Did a Rolling Stone Close Jesus' Tomb?" BAR, September/October 1999. Ya'akov Meshorer, "Ancient Gold Ring Depicts the Holy Sepulchre," BAR, May/June 1986. Jerome Murphy-O'Connor, "The Garden Tomb and the Misfortunes of an Inscription," BAR, March/April 1986. Robert Ousterhout, "The Church of the Holy Sepulchre (in Bologna, Italy)," BAR, November/December 2000.

Resurrection
Michael W. Holmes, "To Be Continued ... The Many Endings of the Gospel of Mark," BR, August 2001. Malcolm L. Peel, "The Resurrection in Recent Scholarly Research," BR, August 1989.

Historical Jesus
John Dominic Crossan, "Why Christians Must Search for the Historical Jesus," BR, April 1996. John P. Meier, "Why Search for the Historical Jesus?" BR, June 1993.